THE ORGANIC BABY
& TODDLER COOKBOOK

Daphne Lambert is an organic chef and nutritionist who has explored the relationship between the food we eat and our health for many years. In 1994 she set up the Penrhos School of Food & Health at mediaeval Penrhos Court on the border of Herefordshire and Wales—her courses cover Pregnancy & Babycare, Women's Health, and Food & Health. She also writes about growing organic food for *Healthy Eating* magazine. Daphne lives with her family at Penrhos, which they have restored over the past twenty-five years into a small organic hotel and restaurant. The restaurant was the first to receive the Soil Association organic symbol.

Formerly a London-based writer on organic issues, **Tanyia Maxted-Frost** now lives with her son Tane in Perth, Western Australia and is Managing Editor of *Homes & Living* magazine. She is also the author of *The Organic Baby Book*. She began her career in New Zealand where she won the Young NZ Journalist of the Year Award in 1984, moving into environmental journalism in Australia in the late 80s.

The Organic Baby & Toddler Cookbook

FROM FIRST FOODS TO FAMILY MEALS

Daphne Lambert
& Tanyia Maxted-Frost

GREEN BOOKS

First published in June 2000
by Green Books Ltd, Foxhole, Dartington,
Totnes, Devon TQ9 6EB

Reprinted with corrections 2002

Cover design by Rick Lawrence

Cover photos of Tane Maxted-Frost and Chloe Mark,
aged 15 months, by photographer Michael Bassett.

Typeset in Sabon and Stone Sans at Green Books

Printed in Great Britain by
J.W. Arrowsmith Ltd, Bristol, UK

A CIP record for this book is available from the British Library.

ISBN 1 870098 86 2

*For simplicity, all babies and toddlers are referred to by the masculine
pronoun ('he'). Apologies to all the little girls out there.*

CONTENTS

Recipes

CONTENTS (continued)

Recipes

For Tane and Hector

Introduction

BABIES AND TODDLERS depend on the food we feed them to grow and develop into fully healthy adults. The quality of the food they eat every day largely determines their state of health—for example, whether they thrive unhindered by illness, or frequently fall victim to colds, gastroenteritis, the 'flu, tonsillitis, or even eczema or asthma, etc.

In the long term, their diet can determine whether or not they become adult victims of heart disease, bowel, breast or prostate cancer or other serious, life-threatening—and avoidable—diseases (at least four out of ten people in the UK now get cancer).

Like any well-functioning engine, little bodies need good fuel, fluids and oil to make them run smoothly and perform well, and to nourish them. A natural, unadulterated organic wholefood diet rich in quality nutrients will provide these, the building blocks for a strong, healthy immune system. In fact the best food you can offer your baby or toddler is organic, home prepared, mainly fresh and raw or lightly cooked, and ideally foods which are in season and have travelled the shortest distance possible.

It is possible to raise a baby or toddler who will be content to eat a piece of raw fruit or a stick of raw cucumber and/or carrot (instead of a bag of crisps or chocolate biscuits), and to happily drink a cup of rice milk or raw carrot juice (instead of sugary cordial or fizzy drinks or even tea!), and for the child to do this and still enjoy the odd wholesome 'sweet' snack without going off his meals. It is also possible to raise a healthy youngster who doesn't feel left out while his friends always eat junk food, or who is typecast as a 'sprouts and lentils' type.

Of course, getting children to eat healthy food is much easier if they grow up expecting it—if it has been their staple diet since weaning, and evident in their mother's milk since birth. Good eating habits and taste preferences are formed early, and while each child is different, it is possible to steer them in the right direction from weaning onwards. As a parent, you have the power to affect the way your child eats throughout his eighteen or so years at home, and probably throughout his whole lifetime.

A parent's lament that a child will only eat junk food is very often self-inflicted and avoidable. Children get poor eating habits from us—it's we parents who buy the food and then hand it to the child or put it on their plate. It's up to us whether we load the shopping trolley with fresh fruit and vegetables, or with packets of crisps, chocolate, biscuits, ice cream and sugary fizzy drinks. It's up to us whether we pull a frozen ready meal out of the freezer each night and throw it in the oven, or prepare fresh, home cooked meals for the dinner table.

Don't believe for a minute that even those 'specially designed' organic baby, toddler and children's foods are any better for them than your own home prepared meals—instead treat these as useful convenience foods when you need to fall back on them, rather than as necessary for your child's diet. Over reliance on any processed food is a recipe for poor health.

WE'VE WRITTEN this book as a guide for parents who want to improve their baby or toddler's health, and who are concerned about pesticide residues, GM foods, antibiotics, artificial sweeteners and other additives which are found in everyday foods. Babies and toddlers are extremely vulnerable to these poisonous chemicals and potential toxins.

We want to encourage parents to get back into the kitchen and give their children the food they actually deserve and that will help them reach their potential. We believe that our values are often misplaced: instead of valuing children's good health highly, and creating it by buying and making the best quality food possible, many parents instead buy them the very cheapest and lowest quality food, but then give them the best toys, clothing, and holidays, and perhaps buy a new family car instead. Priorities are skewed, and people mistakenly believe that it's normal for children to regularly fall sick and have runny noses, and to have a cold or spell in bed every month.

In contrast, parents who raise their children organically report that they are rarely, if ever, sick and are totally or mainly allergy-free. These children are often bigger babies, more robust, and develop quicker—both physically and mentally. Furthermore, a vegan (or dairy-free and animal-free) diet consisting of a mixture of foods that contain both protein and carbohydrate rarely causes digestive problems; these are generally caused by diets containing protein-dense animal products.

We hope that by using this book (ideally in conjunction with *The Organic Baby Book*), you'll be able to make the most of the growing availability and variety of organic food and products, and that, importantly, you'll notice the difference fresh organic can make in the health of your precious little ones. We've certainly noticed the difference in ours.

Daphne Lambert and Tanyia Maxted-Frost

Why Organic?

THERE ARE MANY compelling reasons to give your baby or toddler a mainly organic diet. Here are ten of the best.

• Organic food has been shown in UK, US and European research studies to have **more** vitamins, minerals and other important nutrients such as vitamin C, zinc and secondary metabolites (important plant nutrients) than equivalent conventional food items.

• Organic food is grown **without** poisonous artificial chemical pesticides and fertilisers which leave toxic residues in our food and drinking water. Some of these pesticides have been shown to contribute to or cause cancers, infertility and diseases such as Alzheimer's and Parkinson's.

• Organic food is **free from** the thousands of artificial additives, artificial sweeteners and other 'E numbers' found in conventional foods, many of which are suspected of causing or at least contributing to many diseases including cancer. Health-damaging hydrogenated oils and fats are not permitted in organic foods.

• As organic food production is **stringently controlled** to meet high standards, it is much less likely to be susceptible to the hallmarks of factory farmed food: E coli, salmonella, listeria and other harmful bacteria which cause millions of cases of food poisoning in the UK each year.

• Organic food is certified **GM-free**. If an organic crop is contaminated with genetically modified organisms, the farmer loses his organic certification and the crop cannot be sold as organic.

• Organic food generally **tastes better**—in most taste tests, organic comes out on top. This is because it is unpolluted and has increased levels of nutrients.

• Organic livestock, poultry and fish are **not** fed artificial colourants or animal parts or **routinely** treated with drugs as conventionally reared animals are—**no** cases of BSE have ever been recorded on an organic farm. Organic farming ensures a high standard of animal welfare—animals are are kept in natural environments which allow them to display natural behaviour patterns.

• Organic farming **protects** the environment: it **doesn't** pollute (as conventional farming does), there is no agrochemical drift (since the chemicals aren't used in the first place), nor run-off from artificial pesticides and fertilisers into waterways and drinking water, which kills wildlife and endangers public health. Species such as the skylark, the otter and several species of vole have been pushed to near extinction by intensive farming practices, and pesticides which mimic hormones are thought to have caused fish in our rivers to change sex.

• Organic food labelling tells the full story. There are **no** hidden ingredients whereas there legally can be—and are—in many conventional food labels.

• Organic certification has strictly enforced criteria which ensure that **you can trust the food**. Look for the organic symbol.

Sadly, pesticide residues have been officially found in at least a third of our fresh fruit and vegetables (many containing multiple residues—some up to seven), and in one in eight non-organic babyfood jars. Many prohibited chemicals, such as cancer-causing DDT, have been found in food for sale in the UK; and all oranges, and four out of five UK-grown pears that have been officially tested have been found to contain multiple residues.

An average non-organic diet has been officially found to contain a combination of at least 30 different chemicals, and the government admits that its own testing is underestimating the residue problem in our food by at least 20 per cent.

Babies and toddlers are most at risk from these residues due to their small size as compared to their large food and fluid intake, and the fact that their organs and bodily systems are immature and still rapidly developing.

Other 'nasties' which can be found in conventional foods, and which are behind many of the food scares, include residues of antibiotics and growth hormones, the bacteria E coli, salmonella, and listeria in meat and dairy foods, and genetically modified ingredients in most processed foods. Over 3000 permitted artificial additives can be found in grocery foods, over 50 of which may be of GM origin, and over 55 of which are suspected of causing or contributing to cancer.

ORGANIC AND BIODYNAMIC farming methods produce healthy plants and animals, in a more natural way. This is because they work in harmony with natural systems, rotating crops and pasture, using hedgerows and beetle banks to encourage natural predators of crop pests, and building up and maintaining the fertility of the soil so it is teeming with life and has a good balance of minerals.

Agriculture and food quality are the foundations of public health—only the combination of a healthy organic soil, healthy organic plants, healthy organic animals and an unpolluted environment can help create and sustain healthy people.

For a full, in-depth list of twenty-two good reasons to go organic for a healthy child, see Chapter 1 in *The Organic Baby Book* by Tanyia Maxted-Frost, also published by Green Books.

WHY A MAINLY RAW WHOLEFOOD ORGANIC DIET?

While the methods of producing organic 'fast' food are less harmful to the environment than those of conventional equivalents, the food itself is nowhere near as healthy for you or your child's body as raw, fresh organic wholefoods.

Don't be tricked into thinking that just because food is organic that it's therefore undoubtedly good for you, and healthy: organic crisps, fizzy drinks, chocolate and ice cream may contain less sugar and salt than conventional brands and be free from artificial additives, but they're hardly healthfood.

The organic ingredients in these foods won't have been sprayed with pesticides or dosed with drugs, but food which is processed, cooked and packaged in a factory won't have the nutrients that raw, fresh food has, and there will be increased damage to the environment as a result of the whole packaging process, including its production and waste, transportation, etc.

So wherever possible buy fresh, raw, minimally processed (e.g. wholegrain not white) organic wholefood ingredients and make your own lightly cooked meals. As an added incentive, you'll find that buying fresh is cheaper than buying processed—why pay extra for one type of food which is not as health-promoting as another?

Optimum Nutrition: Towards Organic Health

Optimum nutrition gives the body the best possible intake of nutrients needed for it to function at its optimal level. A varied **organic** wholefood diet, rich in raw fresh fruit and vegetables (both whole and in juices), pulses, wholegrains, cold-pressed oils, seeds and nuts, filtered pure water, and low in (or free from) foods of animal origin, is ideal.

This is because organic food production builds health—it creates balanced levels of natural minerals in the soil, and improves its quality so it teems with life (beneficial micro-organisms). Plants (and animals) produced from this land are therefore as healthy as they can be, giving us optimum nutrition when we eat them as near to their raw state as possible.

We all want the best for our children. So from day one, aim to give them an organic wholefood diet which avoids health-damaging toxins found in conventional foods and allows them to develop optimal mental, emotional and physical performance.

The importance of breastfeeding & building a healthy immune system

Breastfeeding from birth is a vital part of this diet, as breastmilk is the natural designer food for babies, and can be continued into toddlerhood for one to two years, to provide valuable nutrients. If the mother is eating a good organic wholefood diet, her breastmilk will be absolutely premium food.

Breastfeeding lays the foundations for a healthy immune system— able to identify the body's enemies and then destroy them—which is vital for optimum health. If the immune system is compromised in any way, we become susceptible to illness, disease and allergens in childhood and later life.

Two causes of this are eating large amounts of processed foods and sugar, which burden and reduce the effectiveness of our digestive system and leave us deficient in essential nutrients, and regularly consuming pesticide residues and other toxins in our food and fluids.

ORGANIC HEALTH

ORGANIC HEALTH is a natural, optimal state of health and lifestyle to aim for, which is created by optimum nutrition from a balanced, mainly raw and seasonal organic wholefood diet (as detailed on these pages), and from other health-promoting factors such as getting adequate exposure to sunlight, fresh unpolluted air, pure water and natural surroundings such as gardens, woodlands, countryside and coastline.

Aim to integrate and enrich body, mind and spirit: time to play (indulge yourself in a second childhood with your little one and play as a family), take time outdoors (at least half an hour a day and more at weekends), time out to relax and rest, exercise (yoga, walking, cycling, swimming and Pilates are ideal), and socialise and build close relationships with friends and family.

Reduce exposure to potential environmental toxins (see Health Hazards to Avoid on page 26) including unnecessary exposure to radiation (from TV, electrical goods and power transmission lines) and chemicals in household cleaning agents, clothing and bedding (choose environmentally friendly cleaners and avoid synthetic clothes, choosing to wear and sleep in organic or untreated fabric wherever possible). Practice preventative health by boosting your immune system and including Vitamin C and kelp in your diet to remove toxins from your body.

You and your child could eat the best diet, but because of negative factors such as overexposure to pollution, negative attitudes, overwork, resentment, unresolved issues, stress etc., never achieve organic health. Get more balance in your lives, prioritise for health, happiness and wellbeing, and enjoy!

What we eat and drink as babies and toddlers can have a huge influence on our long term health, as poor nutrition in childhood has been shown to cause heart disease, strokes and diabetes in adults.

The strength of our immune system is dependent on an optimal, balanced intake of minerals and vitamins in their natural form. From birth, the first step in building a strong immune system is via colostrum. This is the yellowish transparent fluid that the breast provides before the mature milk comes in. Colostrum contains numerous antibodies to bacteria and viruses. These can help fight infection by polio, mumps, and E. coli. Colostrum also contains a high concentration of zinc, which is essential for a child's growth and development.

A baby's digestive system is far from fully developed in the first few weeks, so the mother's milk is designed to meet its digestive and nutritional needs. As the baby grows, so do his needs, and the mother's milk changes to meet them.

A mother's milk must be as nutritious as possible to ensure that her child is well nourished—especially while he is completely dependent upon it. The foods and fluids she consumes affect the quality of her milk, so she should take great care to eat well (with plenty of fresh enzyme-rich foods), drink plenty of filtered water, exercise gently and rest whenever appropriate while pregnant and breastfeeding her baby.

Breastmilk contains a unique and balanced cocktail of essential minerals, vitamins, hormones, enzymes and antibodies which support the immune system, as well as many other substances we are yet to define. It can never be matched by man-made processed infant formula, but if you have to use formula, choose an organic brand (see *The Organic Baby Book* for product details). Interestingly, research studies have shown breastfed babies to have higher IQs than bottle-fed ones.

Getting it right from weaning— enzymes & other essential nutrients from foods

Long term breastfeeding helps to build a strong, healthy immune system, which further benefits from the appropriate introduction of fresh, nutrient-rich fruits and vegetables.

The first alternatives to breastmilk you should offer your baby between four to six months are fresh raw organic fruit juices, then fresh raw vegetable juices (see Juicing on page 37 for recipes and recommended amounts). These are simple to digest, and contain a concentrated supply of vitamins, minerals, trace elements and beneficial enzymes which are quickly and easily absorbed into the bloodstream.

Enzymes are particularly important for health—when we digest plants in their natural raw state, the enzymes aid the body's digestive system; but they are destroyed when food is cooked. This means that the process of digesting cooked food exhausts the body's reserves, and it has to compensate by working overtime to produce more enzymes both for digestion and other vital functions in the body.

Your long term aim should be to include as much raw fruit and vegetables in your baby or toddler's diet as possible, as this will give his body a greater quantity of these beneficial enzymes and other nutrients than cooked, processed and refined food ever will.

From six to eight months, while your baby's digestive system is still immature, you can start solid weaning foods by steaming or lightly cooking and processing fruit and vegetables into purées to aid digestion (see Fruit Purées & Vegetable Purées on pages 47 and 49). When plant foods are heated, the starch inside the plant's cells swells and ruptures the tough cellulose walls, making the contents accessible and easier for your baby to digest. You will destroy some vitamins and enzymes, but they can instead be provided by breastmilk, and raw fruit and vegetable juices.

Include as many different varieties of fruits and vegetables as possible when weaning your baby (bearing in mind seasonality, etc.). No nutrient works in isolation, so a varied and balanced diet providing all these nutrients is essential (a deficiency of just one vitamin or mineral can suppress the immune system). This approach also means your child will develop a taste for many different foods, and as a result is less likely to become a fussy eater.

Introduce new finger foods (see page 63) at about six to eight months, to encourage chewing and co-ordination. At about eight months, it's time to introduce your baby to blender salads (see page 51). These nutritious combinations include raw fruit or vegetables and are rich in 'immune-boosting' nutrients. The group of nutrients called antioxidants are particularly important, as we need these to keep 'free radicals' in the body in check. Free radicals are dangerous oxidising chemicals which result from poor nutrition and also from various kinds of pollution. They react with and damage many essential parts of our bodies, fight the immune system and cause disease. Beneficial antioxidant nutrients such as beta-carotene (which the body converts into vitamin A), vitamin C and E, bioflavonoids, zinc and selenium, play a vital role, assisting the immune system in disarming free radicals, and enabling the body to maintain health. They also have other immune-boosting functions.

WEANING CHART
FOR OPTIMUM HEALTH

Our recommendations for weaning differ greatly from usual weaning programmes—we advise delaying the introduction of many foods which are difficult for young babies to digest, and suggest introducing non-milk foods firstly as raw juices between four and six months.

This is done to allow the baby's digestive system to accommodate new foods gradually, to lessen the likelihood of allergies, and to increase the ability to pinpoint any allergens. Raw juices, which are rich in enzymes, vitamins and minerals etc., are recommended for life—from weaning.

0–4 months
Breastmilk only, or organic formula milk if unable to breastfeed.

Weaning: 4–6 months
Mainly milk—introduce single, raw organic fruit juices in small amounts (1–2 teaspoons), avoiding acidic fruits (see Juicing, page 37). Give 2–3 small juice tastings a day (10–20 ml each).

Weaning: 6–8 months
Mainly milk—2–3 small fruit juices a day (can now be blends). Introduce simple fruit purées (see page 47)—start with a couple of teaspoons twice a day and build up to 3–4 teaspoons three times a day, and then to suit appetite. Offer a little filtered water between meals.

Introduce single, raw organic vegetable juices in the same amounts as for fruit juices. Slowly introduce mild vegetable juice blends (see Juicing).

Gradually increase amounts of juice intake to 20–30 ml per tasting, two fruit juices and two vegetable juices a day.

Introduce simple vegetable purées (see page 49) in the same amounts as for fruit purées. Alternate fruit and vegetable purées throughout the day. Introduce raw fruit and vegetable finger foods (e.g. slices of apple, pear, carrot and cucumber).

Establishing Solids: 8–10 months
Milk, fruit and vegetable juices and purées, raw finger foods, and a little filtered water. Introduce blender salads (see Ten Blender Salads on page 51).

Approaching Toddlerhood: 10–12 months
Milk, fruit and vegetable juices, filtered water, raw finger foods and three meals a day (see Breakfast, Lunch/Dinner and Puddings recipes from page 52). Also see Finger Foods and Snacks on page 63.

Toddlerhood
As for 10–12 months, but introduce new Savouries & Puddings recipes etc from page 64. Bear in mind that toddlers are often more inclined to graze throughout the day than stick to a three meal format. As this is a perfectly healthy way to eat, ensure your child is getting enough nutrients by ensuring a variety of food and drink as shown in Seasonal Menu Suggestions on pages 104-105.

IMMUNE-BOOSTING FOODS FOR WEANING

During weaning, introduce foods with high levels of vitamin A, C and E, plus the minerals zinc and selenium.

Carrots for vitamin A
Mango for vitamin C
Avocado for vitamin A
Tofu for zinc
Banana for selenium

Vital antioxidant vitamins

Vitamin C is the master immune-boosting nutrient. From the moment a fruit or vegetable is picked, the quantity of vitamin C in it decreases, and every process you subject it to, such as storing, packing and cooking, further reduces its vitamin C content. Locally grown organic sun-ripened fresh fruits and vegetables consumed in their natural raw state will guarantee a rich supply of vitamin C. Particularly high levels are found in broccoli, mange tout, strawberries, blackcurrants, mango, papaya, raspberries, red peppers, sprouted seeds—especially mung beans—and dark green leafy vegetables. (Unfortunately many of our tropical fruits are imported, and imported produce will probably have low amounts of vitamin C due to transport, handling and ageing.)

Vitamin E is another powerful antioxidant which is found in avocados, sweet potatoes, blackberries, mango, tomatoes and watercress.

Beta-Carotene is especially important because it helps to maintain the integrity of the digestive tract, lungs and all cell membranes, preventing germs and viruses from entering cells. It's found in carrots, dark green vegetables, mango, apricot, papayas, pumpkin, sweet potatoes and parsley. Vitamin E and beta-carotene are fat-soluble and therefore not as easily lost as the water-soluble vitamin C.

Vital antioxidant minerals

Selenium Small amounts of selenium are found in most plants, providing it is in the soil—another reason for choosing organic, since intensive farming has seriously lowered levels of selenium in British soils. Nuts (especially Brazil nuts), seeds, seaweed and wholegrains generally have higher levels, which will help compensate for this.

Zinc is found in green vegetables, rice, oats, nuts and seeds. The ideal immune-boosting diet should include plenty of raw fruit and vegetables—especially in the summer—with the addition of a variety of sprouted or cooked grains, seeds and nuts. Saturated and hydrogenated fats should be avoided, but ensure cold-pressed organic seed oils are consumed.

Best sources of vital nutrients

	Two of the best
Protein	Tofu Sunflower seeds
Vitamin B1 (Thiamin)	Oats Potatoes
Vitamin B2 (Riboflavin)	Avocado Wholewheat products
Niacin	Brown rice Dried apricots
Vitamin B6	Wholewheat products Banana
Folic Acid	Oats Broccoli
Vitamin B12	Fortified soya Seaweeds/sprouted seeds
Vitamin C	Red pepper Grapefruit
Vitamin D	Sunshine Green leafy vegetables
Vitamin E	Unrefined cold pressed sunflower oil Dark green leafy vegetables
Vitamin A	Obtained as beta-carotene which is converted in the body to Vitamin A especially from sweet potatoes, carrots and dark green leafy vegetables.
Calcium	Almonds Broccoli
Iron	Apricots Pumpkin seeds
Zinc	Sprouted lentils Miso
Magnesium	Brown rice Sesame

Minerals such as **calcium, magnesium, sodium** and **potassium** are required in large amounts, while others are needed in much lower concentrations (these are called trace minerals and are also found less frequently in the environment and therefore food as well). It is important to feed your baby and toddler good quality organic food, such as fresh fruit, vegetables and unrefined grains, to ensure sufficient levels and a full complement of trace minerals. It is far better to eat a small amount of these than to eat more processed and refined foods (white flour and rice, and foods with sugar), which though high in calories provide little else.

Refined foods may supply energy for a brief while, but they lack the essential trace minerals required for digestion, so our body reserves are used instead—soon the whole body becomes depleted, which makes it vulnerable to disease.

Vitamin D Our most significant supply of Vitamin D comes from the action of ultraviolet–B light on sterols in the skin, although small amounts are available from certain foods (e.g. green leafy plants). Provided your child has plenty of outdoor activity, deficiency is unlikely to be a problem.

Children need healthy fats

Eating the right fat is essential for optimum health. There are three kinds of fat. Saturated fat, found mostly in land animal products and tropical fats like coconut and palm; monounsaturated fats which are found in olives, almonds, avocado and nuts and polyunsaturated fats found in a variety of nuts, seeds, cold water fish and green leafy vegetables. Polyunsaturated fats are the important group for good health. In this group there are two essential fatty acids: linoleic acid (omega 6) and alpha linolenic acid (omega 3).

They are called essential because they are vital to many of the processes in our body yet we are unable to make them ourselves. **Essential fatty acids** are part of all cell membranes, they are involved in transmitting messages between cell and are involved in producing energy in our body from food. They govern growth, vitality and mental state.

To get the maximum health benefits these fats need to be treated with great care as they are fundamentally changed for the worse by light, heat and air (in nature they are packaged in seed cases which exclude these elements) Buy organic, cold pressed oils in dark glass bottles, never heat them but use cold to enrich your food.

The two essential fatty acids need to be in balance in the diet and the best ratio in a healthy body is 3 parts linoleic acid to 1 part alpha linolenic acid. Hemp seed oil has the perfect balance of the two essential fatty acids. You can buy balanced blends like Udo's Choice and Essential Balance which make an excellent addition to your baby or toddler's diet.

- Linoleic acid is found in safflower, sunflower, hemp, soybean,walnut, pumpkin seeds, flax and sesame

- Alpha linolenic acid is found in flax, hemp,soybean, walnut, pumpkin seeds and dark green leafy vegetables.

Menu planning for health

There are a few important considerations when planning menus for your baby or toddler.

- Eat vegetables in season. Generally speaking, foods that grow in spring and summer grow above ground, and according to oriental philosophy are 'cooling' in nature, whereas winter vegetables grow underground and tend to be more 'warming'. Our bodies can benefit from some 'warmth' from our food in cold months and from lighter, 'cooling' foods in spring and summer (see suggested Seasonal Menu Planner on pages 104-105). Consider also the heavy environmental cost of transporting vegetables around the world. Fresh seasonal, local produce is best and natural ripening creates a much higher vitamin content.

- It's best to let your baby or toddler eat when he is hungry. Grazing on small and frequent varied meals with healthy snacks in between is probably best. Listen to what he wants, and let him eat when he is hungry rather than when you think he ought to. Think of it as the 'grazing smörgåsbord' approach: a healthy way for us all to eat. However, don't let him eat constantly—allow adequate time for digestion.

- Eating fruit on its own or at the beginning of a meal makes a lot of sense. Fruit moves through the stomach much faster than protein and carbohydrates. If you eat them together it slows their progress down, causing fermentation, which leads to gas and discomfort. It's best to eat fruit before a meal, as a complete meal, or between meals. Bananas, avocados and apples are an exception to this rule, as they mix well with carbohydrate-rich foods.

• Never be tempted to give your child junk food as a reward or treat, as this sets a dangerous precedent and teaches him that sweet food is special, preferred and good—ahead of 'ordinary' food. Let him have the occasional pudding, cake or biscuit as an integral part of his diet.

KEY POINTS FOR OPTIMUM NUTRITION & ORGANIC HEALTH

1. Breast is best for at least six months, but preferably one to two years (provide high quality milk by eating and drinking high quality fresh organic foods and pure water).

2. Offer only freshly made organic fruit and vegetable juices and filtered water when you wean your baby and throughout childhood (along with nut, rice and soya milks from ten to twelve months on).

3. Serve locally grown and seasonal vegetables and fruits as much as possible, to get maximum nutrients.

4. Use as much raw fruit, vegetables and sprouts as possible, as they contain enzymes and other nutrients which would otherwise be destroyed by cooking and processing.

5. Include as much variety as possible. For protein, choose from lentils, tofu, beans, quinoa, peas, nuts and seeds (ground for children). For carbohydrates, choose from oats, corn, rice, millet, maize, buckwheat, rye and wheat.

6. Provide one serving a day of mineral-rich foods, for example root vegetables, kale, seeds and nuts (ground for children).

7. Use unrefined foods such as wholegrain rice and wholemeal bread, and avoid sugar and processed foods wherever possible.

8. Serve small, high quality meals with healthy snacks in between— it's the quality that counts rather than the quantity.

9. Do not fry in oil—bake or lightly stir fry with sauces instead.

10. Obtain the essential fatty acids from whole foods as much as possible, and use cold-pressed unrefined oils.

11. Add some superfoods to your baby and toddler's meals each day. These can include wheatgrass (see Juicing on page 37), seaweeds (such as Seagreens in condiment form or capsules), garlic, and Udo's oil, Essential Balance or organic hemp oil.

12. Use fresh food as soon as possible and store it correctly to retain nutrients: refrigerate seeds and nuts, and store fruits, potatoes, onions, and garlic in a dark, dry place away from vitamin-reducing light.

Health Hazards to Avoid

As well as eating organic food, there are several other steps you can take to ensure that your young family is as healthy as possible. There are many hazards lurking in your kitchen, and the way you prepare your food can also be detrimental to your child. We've listed some of the key considerations we believe are important.

• **Don't use a microwave.** There are many concerns about the effects of microwave radiation on food and health: scientists warn that microwave ovens promote cancer and destroy vital nutrients. Research has also found that microwaving human milk will destroy its disease-fighting capabilities. In general, microwaves degrade all foods, destroying its vitality—steaming, baking and boiling are better than microwaving. Consuming microwaved food will be detrimental for you and your child's health, and the use of microwaves is now banned in certified organic restaurants and organic catering establishments.

• **Avoid heating plastics**—especially polycarbonate baby bottles and ready-made meal containers made of plastic. International research found that polycarbonate baby bottles leaked the hormone-disrupting chemical bisphenol–A into infant formula milk when heated. To avoid heating them, wash bottles immediately after use in warm soapy water, and heat the milk separately and cool before putting in the bottle. To avoid heating plastic dishes supplied with ready-made meals, put these meals into glass or ceramic oven dishes to heat or bake (or use a glass bowl or a stainless steel steamer inside a saucepan for Christmas puddings etc.).

• **Avoid non-stick frying pans** (which are coated in plastic) or plastic heat-sensitive baby bowls or spoons. Choose a cast iron wok, ceramic pot or stainless steel saucepan instead, and use a stainless steel baby bowl if you're worried about china breaking.

• **Avoid putting plastic cling film** directly on to food, as the plastic softeners can contaminate it. Avoid storing foods in plastic for longer than a couple of days.

• **Avoid products containing hydrogenated fats and oils,** as these create health-damaging trans fatty acids which are linked to mutations, cancers, atherosclerosis and general degeneration of cells, tissues and organs.

- **Avoid using aluminium saucepans** as the toxic metal contaminates food—ceramic or glass is best. The same goes for aluminium foil, which is unfortunately used in some food packaging (even organic).

- **Cow's milk is a common allergen** and is best avoided for at least the first 18 months, or altogether. It contains high levels of a protein called casein—300 times more than in human milk—and once in the stomach it forms large dense curds. The body has to use a huge amount of energy to digest these, leaving less available for other important roles such as supporting the immune system. Additionally, milk and its products are very mucous-forming, and excessive mucous in the body is very detrimental. They are also high in saturated fats and cholesterol, and there are proven links between dairy products and heart disease, arthritis, allergies and migraine. They can also inhibit the absorption of calcium as they coat the intestinal wall over a period of time. If you and your child eat a well balanced wholefood diet rich in nuts, seeds, wholegrains and vegetables, you will obtain enough calcium.

- **Meat products (including poultry)** are also high in saturated fats and cholesterol and **are best kept to a minimum or avoided**. Meat is a concentrated protein, again requiring a huge amount of energy to digest. Protein is actually more readily absorbable from plants. Meat also has no fibre, unlike plants, and is therefore a major cause of constipation. And while fish contain protein, and coldwater fish contain EPA, a derivative of an essential fatty acid—these are also found in plants. Contamination of fish by pollution is becoming an increasing problem for human health. Meat production also exacts a large environmental cost, as does overfishing.

Frequently Asked Questions

How do I make sure my baby or toddler is getting enough calcium, protein and iron?

Breastfeed, and make sure that both you and your child eat a well balanced, varied organic diet, and breastfeed him for at least a year if possible. Eat superfoods such as broccoli, kale, seaweed etc, along with nuts, seeds and beans for protein and calcium. Cut down on dairy foods, which can inhibit calcium absorption, and instead get your calcium from greens, nuts and seeds etc. Vitamin C, which is found in mung beans, fruits and capsicum, increases iron absorption. Iron is found in green leafy vegetables, dried fruit (especially raisins and apricots), wholegrains, dulse, pumpkin, sesame seeds and molasses.

Will my baby or toddler get all the nutrients he needs from his food, or should I give him multivitamin and mineral supplements, and if so, from what age and in what dosage?

If your child lives in a fairly unpolluted area, gets plenty of fresh air, mild sunshine and exercise (once he is mobile), eats a varied, mainly fresh and balanced organic wholefood diet, and is breastfed for 6 months to 1 year or ideally longer, there should not be any need for supplementation. However, if you're unsure about whether to supplement or not it's advisable to see a professional nutritionist or practitioner to review your child's diet and if necessary to recommend supplements. (There are tests available to see whether your child is deficient in vitamins or minerals etc.) If you are going to use supplements, try Nature's Own food state tablets, Higher Nature multivitamins or Biocare powder. These brands have supplements for children and will advise on dosage. Quality supplements will be gluten-, sugar- and dairy-free. Supplementation with a teaspoonful of organic essential fatty acid oil once a day in meals is recommended from weaning—try Udo's Choice or Essential Balance, or a premium organic hemp oil.

Is it alright to give my baby foods and drinks containing sugar or sweetener, and what about the occasional chocolate pudding or cocoa pudding, that some organic babyfood companies now offer?

Sugar is best avoided or kept to a minimum—it is an addictive body poison and encourages the wrong kind of bacteria in the colon. It also causes digestive problems, tooth decay, and can cause hypoglycaemia and diabetes. Sugar calories are empty calories—sugary foods tend to have much lower vitamin and mineral levels. A little honey, organic maple syrup or molasses can be used in place of sugar, but these are also best kept to a minimum as they are not health-promoting. Some artificial sweeteners can cause cancer (among other adverse health effects) and are also best avoided. Unfortunately you'll find them in many drinks and foods aimed at children, so be wary. Chocolate and cocoa contain the powerful stimulants caffeine and theobromine, and are therefore unsuitable for babies and toddlers. Try carob as a healthy alternative.

How do I deal with a fussy eater or hunger striker?

Trust a child's judgement—he will eat when he wants to, and he paces himself. Be laid back—don't make food an issue. Just continue to offer him a little (different) healthy food every now and then at appropriate times, or even offer him something off your plate (as long as he eats it and doesn't just play with it), as your food will often appeal to him more than his – even if it's the same. You could leave a small plate of fresh food out for him to consider on his own. Don't fall into the trap of offering sweet alternatives and convenience foods such as chips in an attempt to get him to eat, as he could end up only eating sweets and chips. The same goes with commercial jar foods. Make food look inviting, and cut down the amount on his plate so it's not overwhelming. With older toddlers involve them (safely) in meal preparation. Make sure that as a family you all sit down together for at least one meal a day (at the table—not in front of the TV), and that you eat when your child eats wherever possible so that he feels part of the action. Try giving him fresh raw juices if he won't eat—he'll be getting liquid food packed with nutrients into his system.

Should I avoid giving my baby wheat and gluten?

These are common allergens so are best avoided for the first year. Gluten, found especially in wheat, but also barley, rye and oats, is like sticky chewing gum in the system—an indigestible glob that adheres to the stomach wall. Rice, buckwheat, millet and maize are good alternatives—make your own gluten-free breads and cereals, or (less preferably) buy them ready-made. Oats have least gluten, and unless diagnosed as coeliac, your child should not have a problem digesting them: it is the high consumption levels of wheat (bred for its high gluten-levels) which particularly overstress our systems and cause digestive problems (including sensitivities to other foods).

How do I get my baby to take water—he's simply not interested and I worry that he'll get dehydrated.

Taking a little filtered water in a drinking cup or bottle regularly is a good habit to get your baby used to—especially in warm weather. Keep offering it to him every now and then, and one day he'll drink it. If you are breastfeeding, your baby shouldn't need extra water or get dehydrated. If you're giving your child raw fresh vegetable and fruit juices, there will be plant water in these, and you can add a little water to drinks to increase his water intake. Try a straw to interest him.

Is fibre good for babies, or is it too much for their systems to cope with?

For babies under a year old, soluble fibres are suitable, such as those in peas, and fruit and vegetable juices, which are also high in vitamins and minerals. Insoluble fibres, such as those in wheat products, are best avoided until your child is over a year old.

Are raw fruits and vegetables hard for my baby to digest?

When juiced these are easy to digest (see the chapter on Juicing for recommendations from four months). First purées can be steamed or lightly cooked to aid digestion, but by six to eight months your baby will be able to tolerate some raw foods, and ideally, as he grows older, the more fresh raw food he has the better.

If I let my one year old feed himself, it's like a food fight and everyone and everything close by gets covered. I worry that he's not getting the nutrients he needs, as he refuses to take it off the spoon. What shall I do?

It's been said that the best place to let a baby learn to feed himself is in a car wash! Let him feed himself once a day, to allow him to develop his co-ordination, and then feed him yourself for other meals; or try feeding him a spoonful and then letting him hold the next spoonful and guide it in himself. Just be patient, firm and consistent, and he'll get the hang of it eventually. Keep the raw juices and breastmilk going and he won't be missing out on any nutrients.

My toddler has suddenly stopped fitting into set meal times and now seems more content with several smaller meals throughout the day. Is this OK or should I try to get him back into the three meals a day pattern?

Go with it—your toddler is listening to his body and eating little and often (in effect, grazing), which is best for balancing blood sugar and energy needs throughout the day and aiding proper digestion and absorption. It gives you the opportunity to offer him a variety of foods— we call it the 'grazing smörgåsbord' approach to eating, which is healthy for us all, providing there is adequate time for digestion between snacks.

Other considerations

- Try not to make food an issue or a battleground. Don't use sweets or chips as bribery or place great emphasis on these foods as treats or reward, as you'll create a child who prefers sweets and chips to 'ordinary' food.

- Treat eating as a family pastime, encourage social interaction at the dinner table and celebrate being a family.

- As soon as your child is old enough involve him in food preparation. It is the most important and vital part of his life and it's up to you to teach him—you certainly can't rely on the education system to do this!

Setting Up
an Organic Kitchen

Useful kitchen equipment

(Recommended brands are marked in italics)

Juicer The most important piece of equipment you will ever buy *(Champion, Green PowerPlus)*.

Wheatgrass juicer If your existing juicer does not juice wheatgrass, you will need to buy one *(Green Leaf, Porkert)*.

Food processor Makes all sorts of work effortless *(Moulinex)*.

Coffee grinder A small electric coffee grinder comes in very handy for grinding small quantities of nuts and seeds (can be an attachment to some food processors such as *Moulinex*).

Food dehydrator Not essential but really useful to make enzyme-rich food in place of cooked.

Drinking water filter Ideally a plumbed-in reverse-osmosis water filter system *(Freshwater Filter, Aquathin)*.

Steamer Quick and easy way to cook vegetables. Stainless steel.

Chopping boards Made from Forestry Stewardship Council wood.

Stainless steel saucepans Never use aluminium.

Cast iron wok   For quick, simple dishes (the iron can also help overcome any iron deficiency).

Cast iron frying pan   For pancakes and griddle cakes (again the iron can also help overcome any iron deficiency).

Sharp knives   Worth investing in good ones to make cutting vegetables easy and safe.

Garlic press   Not essential as you can crush with a knife.

Large wide-mouth glass jars
For sprouting seeds, pulses, beans etc. Cover with net & rubber bands or use a ready made glass sprouter *(Eschenfelder, Living Sprouts)*.

Cafeteria style trays   For growing green sprouts (not plastic).

Rubber ice cube trays   Excellent for freezing babyfoods.

Freezing containers   For storing the cubes.

Bags   For freezing.

Greaseproof paper & tape
For wrapping up food before bagging and freezing.

Airtight containers   For storing foods in fridge.

Organic store cupboard

(Brands the authors use are marked in italics
—try local alternatives where available)

Oils
- Cold pressed olive oil*
  (Meridian)
- Cold pressed, sesame, hemp,
  walnut, hazelnut, pumpkin*
  oils *(Meridian, Elmers)*
- Essential fatty acid blend*
  *(Udo's Oil, Essential
  Balance, Organic Hemp Oil
  from Mother Hemp, Omega)*

Nuts
- Walnut*
- Almond*
- Hazelnut*
- Coconut (shredded)*

Seeds
- Hemp*
- Flax*
- Sunflower*
- Sesame*
- Pumpkin*

Dried Fruits
- Apricots
- Raisins
- Prunes
- Dates
- Sultanas

Seeds (for sprouting)
- Alfalfa
- Buckwheat
- Fenugreek
- Chickpea
- Lentil
- Sunflower
- Wheat
- Mung

Pulses (for cooking)
- Chickpea
- Aduki
- Haricot
- Pinto
- Black bean
- Split lentils
- Lentils

Wholegrains
- Pot barley
- Millet
- Rice
- Quinoa

Sea Vegetables
- Nori
- Dulse
- Kombu
- Arame
- Wakame
- Also ground seaweed as
  condiment or capsules
  (Seagreens, Green People)

Drinks
- Rice Milk (*Rice Dream, Clearspring*)
- Soya milk *(Provamel, Bon Soy)*
- Coffee substitute *(Bambu)*
- Herbal teas *(Hambleden Herbs, Clipper, Yogi Bhajan)*

Sundries
- Soya sauce (tamari) *(Clearspring)*
- Vegetable bouillon *(Marigold)*—see how to make your own stock on pages 106-107.
- Flour *(Dove's, Pimhill)*
- Polenta *(Biona)*
- Miso *(Clearspring, Source Foods)*
- Ginger root
- Parsley
- Garlic
- Molasses *(Meridian)*
- Honey *(Rowse, NZ honey)*
- Seed mustard *(De Rit)*
- Olives
- Coconut milk/cream
- Tofu *(Dragonfly, Oasis, Clearspot, Cauldron Foods)*
- Tempeh *(Source Foods)*

Convenience Foods
- Rice cakes *(Kallo)*
- Rice crackers *(Sanchi, Wakame)*
- Breakfast cereals *(Ecobaby, Whole Earth, Nature's Path, Infinity, Dove's Multiflake)*
- Baked beans *(Whole Earth)*
- Udon & soba noodles *(Clearspring)*
- Wholewheat pasta *(Meridian, La Terra e Il Cielo)*
- Bread *(The Village Bakery, Stamp Collection)*
- Pitta bread
- Prepared tomato/pasta sauces *(Meridian, Whole Earth, Go Organic)*
- Tahini *(Meridian)*
- Peanut butter *(Meridian, Whole Earth)*
- Baby rusks *(Kallo)*
- Instant miso soup *(Source Foods, Sanchi)*

Spices *(Hambleden Herbs)*
- Cinnamon
- Coriander
- Cloves
- Cumin
- Nutmeg
- Herbs de Provence

* Store in the fridge

Recipes

The recipes and menu suggestions featured in this book have been specially created to include a wide range of organic ingredients that will provide your child with the best possible variety of nutrients as he needs them. Try to include fruit at every breakfast meal, and a salad or raw vegetables at every lunch and dinner. Vary the meals as much as possible from day to day (see the Seasonal Meal Planner on pages 104-105). As soon as your child is old enough, let him help prepare the meals.

Juicing

Drinking raw, fresh fruit and vegetable juices is the best and quickest way to get all of the valuable minerals, vitamins, enzymes and other nutrients found in these healthy organic foods into your baby's body and your own. As the fibre has been removed during the juicing process, these nutrients are easily absorbed, and as they are fresh, are far superior to any processed and packaged vitamin and mineral supplement or processed juice you can find on shop shelves.

Single fruit juices are suitable for babies from weaning, and single vegetable juices can be introduced as your baby reaches four months. As being a parent is a tiring, full time job, fresh juices can also help to revitalise you, and keep you healthy and energised to cope with all the demands that baby and toddler, and your new role, will inevitably place on you. Juices are excellent for both parents preparing to conceive a baby, and for mum during pregnancy, breastfeeding, and beyond!

To get the most out of juicing, bear in mind that as soon as a fruit or vegetable is harvested it begins to deteriorate, and that storage, transportation and handling will further diminish its nutritional content. Choose muddy root vegetables rather than washed ones, as the mud helps to preserve the nutritional value. Extracting the juice from freshly picked food and drinking the juice straight away is the most efficient way to use all of the available nutrition. Maximum nutrition will therefore come from seasonal locally grown fruit and vegetables. However, it's far easier to keep to local seasonal vegetables than fruits, as everyone loves delicious tropical fruits such as bananas, pineapples, mango, paw-paw and oranges, but we just can't grow them in this country.

With all juices, store your ingredients well in a cool and dark place to preserve them, gather them together as you are about to juice, and only then wash and chop them into suitable size pieces for your juicer. Don't be tempted to cut them up in advance and put them aside, or make the juice before you are ready to drink it, as many nutrients will be lost in the process; and as they are organic, leave fruits and vegetables unpeeled wherever possible as the skin and the flesh directly underneath contain vital nutrients which would otherwise be lost. Just wash, chop, juice, drink and enjoy!

Juices for Mum

Include as many raw, fresh organic juices in your diet as possible—ideally two vegetable and one fruit a day (especially while pregnant or breastfeeding) as the fantastic benefits of the vitamins, minerals, enzymes and other easily absorbed nutrients will be immediately passed on to your baby. Particularly recommended are the juices of carrots, apples, beetroot, cucumber and watercress.

Also consider growing your own wheatgrass and alfalfa at home and juice these as well—it's easy once you have a system going (see Sprouting on page 44), and is a cheap way of getting nutrient-rich greens into your daily diet. These 'super' greens contain all essential vitamins, minerals and enzymes, and because they are sprouted, they are bursting with natural energy and health-promoting chlorophyll. Wheatgrass is a great blood purifier; it enters the bloodstream extremely quickly, so introduce it slowly into your diet. Juicing these greens enables you to consume a lot more of them and their nutrients than you would if you ate them normally, and allows you to use them quickly while they are at their peak so no nutrients are lost while they languish in the back of the fridge.

Use combinations of the following juice recipes every day—up to two pints of vegetable juice and one pint of fruit juice, plus one to two daily boosters.

SUPER VEGETABLE JUICE RECIPE

1 handful alfalfa sprouts
2 carrots—unpeeled and well scrubbed
1 beetroot—small unpeeled beetroot preferably with tops, well scrubbed
2 sticks celery
$1/2$ red pepper
1 chunk cucumber
$1/2$ fennel bulb
2 or 3 sprigs watercress
1 piece of ginger, unpeeled and washed
2 cloves garlic

Nutritional information
on Super Juice recipe

Alfalfa   Contains all the essential minerals, and is rich in zinc and iron
Beetroot   High in iron and silica, it assists regeneration of red blood cells
Carrots   Contain large amounts of beta-carotene, which the body
               turns into vitamin A
Celery   Rich in zinc, potassium and sodium
Cucumber   High in potassium, phosphorus, iron and silica
Red pepper   Loaded with vitamin C
Watercress   Rich in iron, iodine and potassium
Fennel   Stimulates milk flow in breastfeeding mums; good for the
               digestive system
Ginger   Anti-inflammatory and promotes healing
Garlic   Natural antibiotic

DAILY BOOSTERS

Fresh, freeze-dried or powdered wheatgrass juice (1oz, or 1 teaspoon) with a small carrot juice (if you can't grow your own, try freeze-dried Sweet Wheat from Xynergy).

and/or

Freshly juiced: 1 peeled lemon, 2 unpeeled apples and 1 clove of garlic (peeled and crushed).

FRUIT JUICES

Spring Refresher
6 sprigs of mint, 1 peeled lemon, 2 unpeeled kiwi, 1 unpeeled pear, 1 unpeeled apple

Summer Glory
8 oz strawberries, 2 stoned and quartered peaches, 4 oz blackcurrants

Autumn Marvel
8 oz raspberries, 2 quartered apples, 6 oz red grapes

Winter Warmer
1 peeled pineapple, 2 unpeeled pears, 1 oz root ginger

All Year Round Lemon Aid
1 peeled lemon, 4 unpeeled apples

Fruit Smoothie
2 peeled oranges, 1 peeled mango, 2 passionfruit (scooped out flesh of), 1 frozen banana

For the smoothie, juice the orange and passionfruit only, and then blend in a food processor with the mango flesh and the banana. To freeze bananas, peel when ripe, cut into chunks and freeze on a tray. Pop into a bag and secure and keep in the freezer until ready to use.

You can make an extra cold fruit smoothie for hot months by using frozen mango or frozen strawberry chunks either on their own, together, or combined with frozen banana chunks homogenised in your juicer (the Champion is ideal for this), or blended in a food processor.

Weaning juices for baby

Between four to six months is the time to start introducing your baby to different tastes and foods using raw, fresh fruit juices. Introduce these gradually and individually as a tasty addition to mother's milk (or formula if you're unable to breastfeed). Start with a teaspoon or two of apple juice, then try pear and then maybe grape. Wash the fruit for juicing, but leave unpeeled if organic. If in season, strawberry and apricot juices are delicious. Avoid acidic juices such as orange and grapefruit, and ensure that the fruit is ripe, to aid digestion. Once your baby is happily taking the juice off a spoon, give him small amounts in a drinking cup or bottle. Two small tastings (10-20 ml each) a day is ample at this stage. From six to eight months you can try fruit juice blends as well as single juices.

When you move your baby on to vegetable juices at around six to eight months, start with carrot (leave unpeeled if organic) and slowly introduce different blends for older babies with carrot as a base including red and yellow pepper, celery, beetroot, fennel, and a very little alfalfa and wheatgrass. It's important to incorporate these slowly into the diet, and with only a very little at a time. If your baby finds juices too strong, add a little filtered water. Again, try a different flavour on a teaspoon initially, and then in a drinking cup or bottle. Three to four small tastings of fruit and vegetable juices a day is ample (start with 10–20 ml and work up to 20–30 ml per tasting), although your baby may want a little more than this by eight months, which is fine. It's also a good idea to get your older baby used to drinking a small amount of filtered water each day in a drinking cup or bottle, especially during summer.

Juices for older babies & toddlers

Encourage your older baby and toddler into the good habit of having 1/4 to 1/2 a drinking cup of raw fresh fruit juice in the morning, and 1/4 to 1/2 a cup of raw fresh vegetable juice in the afternoon. Juicing is a good habit for life, and replaces reliance on commercial, processed drinks which won't be as nutrient-rich or fresh. In fact even many organic juices on the shelves are made from concentrate.

If you're juicing regularly, your little one will get used to hearing the juicer and anticipate the fresh, flavoursome concoction he's about to receive. And if you lead by example, drinking fresh juices yourself, he'll understand that they're an everyday part of family life.

If you have a fussy drinker, try a straw.

Try some of the following juice recipes and rotate them. (Also see menu suggestions for your toddler, which include juices.)

Morning
3–4 apples
   or
3–4 pears
   or
Part of watermelon (in season)

Afternoon
2 carrots, $^1/_2$ red pepper, $^1/_2$ yellow pepper (alternate with cucumber and celery, including the tops), or a smaller, diluted version of the Super Vegetable Juice or Vegetable Daily Booster recipes on page 38.

Sprouting Chart

Seed type	Soak for	Sprout for	Tips
Nuts	12 hours		Soaking removes enzyme inhibitors. Store in fridge in water. Change water daily.
Hulled pumpkin	6 hours	2 days	
Hulled sunflower	6 hours	2 days	
Hulled sesame	4 hours	1 day	Very bitter if the sprouts are grown long
Hulled buckwheat	15 mins	2–3 days	
Wheat	8 hours	3 days	
Mung	12 hours	4 days	Grow in the dark
Chickpeas	12 hours	3–4 days	A complete protein
Green lentils	8 hours	3–4 days	Superb, easily assimilated protein
Alfalfa	6 hours	5 days	Remember to develop chlorophyll by growing in sunlight for at least 12 hours
Red clover	6 hours	5 days	
Fenugreek	6 hours	5 days	Delicious and spicy
Peas	8 hours	3 days	
Pinto bean	12 hours	3 days	
Aduki	12 hours	3 days	Grow in the dark

Sprouting times will vary according to season and room temperature.

Weaning: 4–8 months
Sprouting

Home grown sprouts are easy, cheap and fun to grow—they can be grown on a kitchen windowsill, but most important of all they are extremely nutritious. As seeds germinate, they spring into life and become more nutritious for humans. The enzyme inhibitors, phytates and oxalates present in every seed, nut or grain are removed when sprouting occurs. Starches are converted into simple sugars. Proteins and fats are broken down into an easily digestible form, and vitamins are synthesised.

Sprouting gives you a ready supply of fresh greens which can be used in juices, salads and vegetable blends. They contain many essential vitamins, minerals and enzymes needed by growing babies and toddlers. From seed to edible sprout takes 1–5 days (see sprouting chart). You can sprout alfalfa, wheatgrass, beans, seeds and pulses.

Method

Choose a large jar (or a purpose-made sprouting jar—see Information Sources on page 109), put in your chosen seed or bean, cover with filtered water, and then fasten a piece of fine net over the top using a rubber band. After soaking for the appropriate time, pour off the soak water and rinse the seeds well. Turn the jar upside down and let it drain. Rinse the sprouts morning and evening. It is important to keep them moist, warm (room temperature is fine) and well drained. Between rinsing, place the jars at an angle for easy drainage.

Once the sprouts are ready, rinse thoroughly in a colander, drain, put in a bowl, cover and store in the fridge. It's important to:

1. Put alfalfa in the sunlight for 12 hours to develop the chlorophyll.

2. Grow mung beans and aduki in the dark for best results. The secret to long straight and juicy mung bean sprouts is to grow them under pressure. One way to do this is to grow them in a colander with a heavy plate and jar of water on top.

Wheatgrass

Some sprouts are grown on trays to develop leaves—the most important being wheatgrass—but you can also grow buckwheat and sunflower sprouts in the same way. These tray-grown sprouts are rich in chlorophyll, the health benefits of which are considerable. Wheatgrass is a great blood purifier and cleanser, and enters the bloodstream extremely quickly.

It is extremely easy to grow (see below). Once it is seven days old, cut the grass and extract the juice. (Not all juicers extract wheatgrass juice— see page 110.) There are many benefits of drinking wheatgrass juice, as wheatgrass:

- Has one of the richest sources of vitamins A and C
- Contains a balanced range of B vitamins
- Contains a balanced amount of calcium, phosphorus, magnesium, sodium and potassium
- Provides iron to the blood to improve circulation
- Contains 92 trace minerals
- Is 70% chlorophyll
- Reduces blood pressure
- Purifies the liver
- Relieves constipation
- Improves blood sugar problems
- Acts as a disinfectant by killing off bacteria in the blood lymph and various tissues.

Freshly squeezed wheatgrass juice is a powerful cleanser. Wheatgrass juice may initially cause nausea—this is a reaction to wheatgrass juice encountering toxins in your system. Adults should drink only very small amounts and build up to a maximum of 2 oz a day. Babies and toddlers should be given only a few drops, gradually working up to a teaspoon a day.

Materials:
2 cafeteria style trays 10" x 12" or 14" x 18"
Organic compost and ordinary top soil (50%/50%)
Soaked organic wheatgrass seeds (for source see page 111)

1. After soaking the seeds drain into a colander, rinse well and leave to germinate for 12 hours. Keep covered to retain moisture.

2. Mix the soils together and cover the tray with the mixture. Moisten the soil so it is wet but not soggy.

3. Spread the seeds evenly on the tray.

4. Place the other tray on top to hold in the moisture.

5. Keep an eye on the tray and water if required.

6. After three days the top tray will start to lift off. Uncover, water thoroughly and place in a bright spot. Your wheatgrass will be ready to harvest four days later.

Once you've juiced the wheatgrass, drink it within 10 minutes. Cut grass will store for a week in a bag in the fridge. Frozen wheatgrass will keep for a month, but is not as effective as freshly made juice.

Compost the soil in the tray after harvesting the sprouts. This recycled soil should be ready to use again in about three months.

Grow buckwheat and sunflower seeds in the same way. Harvest and use abundantly in salads, and also juice.

Fruit Purées

Simple, single raw or lightly cooked fruit purées are ideal for introducing solids to your baby once he has tasted and grown used to simple raw fruit juices. To start with, just offer a couple of teaspoons of purée twice a day to get him used to the texture and tastes, and gradually build up to 3–4 teaspoons three times a day, and then to suit his appetite. Cooled leftovers or extra amounts can be frozen in icecube trays which can be conveniently popped out to thaw and use, or covered and stored in the fridge for use the next day. Try the following suggestions.

APPLE

Wash, peel, core and chop 3 small ripe apples such as Cox's. Place in a small saucepan with water, bring to the boil and simmer until tender and then purée. Makes 4 servings.

For a cool, raw purée on a warm day, simply blend apples and serve.

APRICOT (DRIED)

Soak 6 apricots overnight in water. Place in a small saucepan with the water, bring to the boil, cover, and simmer until tender and then purée. Makes 4 servings.

BANANA

Mash 1 very ripe banana, adding soya milk or rice milk to make a smooth consistency.

MANGO

Take 1/2 ripe mango and purée into a smooth consistency. Makes 1 serving.

PAPAYA

Take ½ ripe papaya and purée into a smooth consistency. Makes 1 serving.

PEAR

Wash, peel and core 1 ripe pear, then purée to a smooth consistency. You can add a teaspoon of lemon juice as desired. Makes 1 serving.

PEACH

Peel and stone 3 ripe peaches. Chop and put into a saucepan with a little water, cover, and simmer until tender and then purée. Makes 4 servings.

PLUM

Cook 6 ripe plums with water until very tender, then sieve to remove the stones. Purée. Makes 3 servings.

PRUNES

Cover 1 dozen stoned prunes with water and soak overnight. Boil and simmer for 20 minutes. Purée to a smooth consistency. Kept in the fridge, this will last for a week. Makes 8 servings.

STRAWBERRY

Take ½ dozen ripe strawberries and purée to a smooth consistency. Makes 1 serving.

Vegetable Purées

Once your baby has tried vegetable juices, introduce texture with vegetable purées, and gradually intersperse these with the fruit purées throughout the day. Freeze as icecubes or refrigerate extra servings and leftovers once cool.

SWEET POTATO

2 medium sweet potatoes peeled and sliced

Place the sweet potato in a steamer and steam for 15 minutes. Transfer to a food processor and purée.

POTATO

1 large potato washed

Bake the potato in the centre of a medium oven for 45 minutes.
Split open, scrape out the middle and mash using a fork with a little virgin olive oil and chopped parsley. (Cook several potatoes together and use the rest for family meals to conserve energy.)

PARSNIP

2 medium parsnips, peeled and sliced

Place the parsnip in a steamer and steam for 15 minutes. Transfer to a food processor and purée. Add 2 teaspoons of tahini (ground sesame seed paste).

CARROT

2 medium carrots, scrubbed and sliced

Place the carrots in a steamer and steam for 15 minutes, transfer to a food processor and purée.

BROCCOLI

2 medium heads of broccoli

Cut off the hard stalk, place in a steamer, steam for about 10 minutes then purée.

SWEETCORN

1 fresh corn on the cob.

Strip the heads off the cob, put in a minimal amount of water and boil until tender, purée with the cooking water.

PEAS

1 cup of fresh or frozen peas. Fresh are superior but frozen peas are a very popular convenience food. Fresh peas will need to be cooked longer than frozen, then purée with the cooking water.

Ten Blender Salads

These blends contain a mix of essential nutrients your growing baby needs, so rotate them. Blend up more than you need and refrigerate, or use leftovers in your own meal. With tofu, make your own or buy large blocks and keep in an airtight container—just cut off what you need each time. Choose chilled, fresh tofu rather than the long life version, and be aware of the use-by date.

1. Tofu, steamed broccoli, grated raw carrot

2. Raw avocado and alfalfa sprouts

3. Tofu, tahini and fresh carrot juice

4. Tofu, raw banana and soaked apricot

5. Tofu, steamed sweet potato and chopped raw watercress

6. Raw avocado, papaya and mango

7. Tofu, steamed parsnip and fresh or freeze-dried wheatgrass juice

8. Raw avocado, watercress and steamed carrot

9. Raw avocado and cooked peas or steamed broccoli

10. Tofu with steamed butternut squash, fresh parsley, ginger and garlic

Breakfast

Breakfast is an important meal for growing babies reaching toddlerhood, as they get more mobile and require a good start to the day. Try varying this morning meal as much as possible. Offer a fresh fruit juice.

MUESLI

1 tbsp porridge oats
1 dessertspoon Udo's oil

Breast or soya milk (about 4 tbsp)
1 dessertspoon apple purée

Soak the oats overnight in the milk in the fridge. Stir in the oil and the apple and serve.

BANANA PORRIDGE WITH SESAME

1 tsp well-ground sesame seeds
1 oz porridge oats

$^1/_3$ pint soya milk
1 small banana

Grind sesame seeds using a grinding attachment on a food processor or a separate manual grinder, and simmer gently in a small pan with the soya milk and oats until creamy. Mash the banana, stir in and simmer for another minute.

POLENTA WITH SULTANAS & MAPLE SYRUP

2 oz polenta
$^1/_2$ oz sultanas

$^1/_2$ pint water
Maple syrup

Bring the water to the boil. Steadily pour in the polenta, beating well all the time. Add the sultanas and cook for 1 minute. Serve in a bowl with a little maple syrup.

COUSCOUS WITH COCONUT & MASHED BANANA

$^1/_2$ pint milk
1 tsp coconut cream
Pinch of cinnamon

1 heaped tablespoon couscous
1 banana

Heat the milk and couscous together for 10 minutes until thick, add the coconut cream and pour into a bowl. Serve topped with mashed banana and cinnamon.

MANGO & RASPBERRY SOUP

1 orange
4 oz raspberries

1 small mango
Mint sprig

Juice the orange. Peel the mango and cut the flesh from the stone. Purée the mango with the orange juice and pour into a bowl. Purée and sieve the raspberries. Swirl the raspberry purée through the mango purée and serve.

APPLE SLICES WITH FRUIT DIP

Slice the apple so that it's easy for your baby to hold, dip and chew. To make the dips, blend fruit ingredients together in a food processor. Choose from:

Fig & Orange
8 dried figs marinaded overnight in fresh orange juice with the pulp

Banana & Peach
$1/2$ frozen banana, 1 fresh peach and the juice of $1/2$ orange

Date & Vanilla
4 oz dates soaked overnight in apple juice with a split vanilla pod

Prune & Ginger
8 prunes soaked overnight in water with a teaspoon of grated ginger

Pear & Banana
$1/2$ frozen banana, 1 pear and 6 strawberries

Lunch & Dinner

Variety will keep your older baby interested and ensure he's getting all the nutrients he needs. All recipes serve four. Offer a fresh vegetable juice. Refer to page 106 for instructions on making your own stock.

ASPARAGUS SOUP

2 oz olive oil
1 medium potato, peeled & diced
1 pint vegetable stock

2 medium onions, chopped
1¹/₂ lb asparagus

Discard the tough bottoms of the asparagus, pare off any stringy bits and cut the remainder into small pieces. Gently cook the onions in the olive oil, then add the potatoes, asparagus and the stock. Simmer for 30 minutes. Blend the soup until smooth and serve.

SWEET POTATO SOUP

1¹/₂ pints vegetable stock
2 large sweet potatoes, peeled & diced
2 sticks celery, chopped
2 cloves garlic, peeled & crushed

2 medium carrots, diced
1 medium onion, diced
¹/₂ teaspoon cumin seeds
¹/₂ teaspoon ginger, grated

Heat stock, add all the remaining ingredients and simmer for 20 minutes. Blend the soup until smooth and serve.

MISO SOUP WITH VEGETABLES

1 pint water	1 corn cob kernels, cut off
1 diced carrot	1 diced onion
1 clove garlic, peeled & crushed	1 teaspoon grated ginger
2 oz watercress, finely chopped	2 oz broccoli florets
2 oz tofu	2 tablespoons miso

Bring the water to the boil and add the corn, carrot, onion, garlic and ginger, and simmering for 10 minutes. Add the watercress, broccoli and tofu, cooking for a further 5 minutes. Strain the liquid into a clean pan. Process the solids to a textured purée and return to the cooking liquid with 2 tablespoons of miso.

Miso
Miso is a fermented soya bean paste which is rich in digestive enzymes and high in protein. Don't cook above 65°C, as this will destroy the beneficial enzymes.

CORN SOUP

2 cobs of corn, kernels cut off	½ pint vegetable stock
1 teaspoon miso	1 teaspoon chopped chives
1 teaspoon chopped parsley	

Blend the corn, vegetable stock and miso until creamy. Add the herbs and serve. Children love the colour of this cold soup.

PEA & MINT DIP

2 spring onions
2 tbsp olive oil
4 sprigs mint

2 cloves garlic, peeled
8 oz fresh peas (or frozen)
1 teaspoon lemon juice

Gently soften the onions and garlic in the olive oil and 2 tablespoons of water, add the peas and cook very gently for 2 minutes if frozen, 5 minutes if fresh. Pour the mixture into a blender and blend with the fresh mint and lemon juice. Can be served with toasted rye bread (see page 95).

COURGETTE & RICE CAKE

6 oz risotto rice
6 oz courgette
1 carrot, grated
1 tsp coconut cream
2 oz tofu

1 tbsp olive oil
1 onion, grated
1 clove garlic, finely diced
2 tbsp soya milk

Cook the rice in boiling water for 10 minutes and drain. Cook the vegetables in the oil for 5 minutes and mix with the rice. Blend together the coconut cream, soya milk and tofu, add to the mixture and stir well. Turn into an oiled tin and bake for 15–20 minutes at 180°C (350°F, gas mark 4) until golden. Serve in wedges.

RED RICE & TOMATO PILAFF

1 tbsp olive oil
5 oz red rice
4 tomatoes, skinned and seeded

2 cloves garlic, peeled & chopped
1½ pints vegetable stock
2 tbsp chopped parsley

Cook the garlic gently in the oil, add the rice, pour on the stock and simmer for 35 minutes. Stir in the tomatoes and parsley five minutes from the end. Mash slightly if required and serve.

BARLEY & VEGETABLE CASSEROLE

2 cloves garlic, peeled & chopped   2 tbsp olive oil
1 onion, diced   2 small carrots, diced
1 small parsnip, diced   2 sticks celery, diced
2 oz pot barley   1 pint vegetable stock

Cook the garlic gently in the oil, add the vegetables, stir for 2 minutes, add the barley and the stock. Simmer gently for 40 minutes, mash slightly if required and serve.

GUACAMOLE

3 ripe avocados   ½ small grated onion
2 cloves garlic, peeled and crushed 2 tsp lime juice
1 tbsp olive oil   .   Cayenne pepper

Cut the avocados in half, remove the stones and scoop out the flesh. Mash the flesh with the onion and garlic, then mix in the lime juice, olive oil and cayenne pepper. Serve with sticks of celery or carrot.

BUCKWHEAT RISSOLES

6 oz buckwheat   2 tbsp olive oil
1 onion, finely chopped   1 carrot, finely chopped
1 clove garlic, peeled &   1 chunk ginger, grated
1 tbsp wholemeal flour   2 tsp tamari
1 tsp each of ground sesame, pumpkin & sunflower seeds

Cook the buckwheat in simmering water until soft (approximately 15 minutes). Meanwhile gently cook the onion, carrot, garlic and the ginger in the oil until soft. Drain the buckwheat and add to the vegetable mix along with the remaining ingredients. When cool enough to handle, shape into small rissoles, arrange on a greased baking tray and bake for 15 minutes at 180°C (350°F, gas mark 4).

POLENTA

1 tbsp olive oil
1 clove garlic, chopped
9 oz polenta

1 onion, chopped
1¹/₂ pints of stock

Gently cook the onion and garlic in the oil until soft but not coloured. Add the stock, bring to the boil, and slowly pour in the polenta, beating well. Cook briefly and pour into an oiled tin to set. Cut into fingers and bake at 180°C (350°F, gas mark 4) for 10 minutes.

QUINOA PILAFF

8 oz quinoa
1 onion, finely chopped
¹/₂ tsp paprika
2 oz raisins
2 tsp finely chopped parsley

1 pint vegetable stock
2 tbsp olive oil
¹/₂ tsp cumin
1 oz soaked dried apricots, finely sliced

Cook the quinoa in the stock for about 15 minutes. While it cooks gently, soften the onion in the olive oil on medium heat, add the spices and cook together for a further 30 seconds. Add the raisins and the apricots. Strain the quinoa when it is ready and stir in the onion and fruit mixture. Put into a bowl, sprinkle with the parsley and serve.

MILLET RISOTTO

9 oz millet (soaked for 4 hours)
4 oz peas
3 oz red peppers, diced
1 red onion, diced

1 pint vegetable stock
4 oz carrots, diced
1 courgette, diced

Rinse the millet well, place with the stock in a pan and bring to the boil. Lower the heat, add the vegetables and simmer for 5 minutes. Remove from heat and let sit for 10 minutes before fluffing up and serving.

MILLET CAKES WITH SESAME GARLIC DIP

4 oz millet
1 clove garlic, peeled & crushed
1 tbsp parsley, chopped
1 carrot, grated

1 pint vegetable stock
1 onion, diced
2 tbsp alfalfa sprouts, chopped
1 spring onion, finely chopped

Cook the millet in the stock, with the garlic and onion for 20 minutes. Cool slightly, add all the remaining ingredients and shape into cakes. Bake on an oiled tray in a hot oven (220°C, 425°F, gas mark 7) for 5–10 minutes.

Serve with sesame-garlic dip, made by blending together:

3 tbsp olive oil
1 tbsp lemon juice
2 tbsp water
1 tsp parsley, chopped

2 cloves garlic, peeled
2 tbsp tahini
1/2 tsp chives, chopped

POTATO CAKES WITH SEAWEED

2 large potatoes
8 oz oats
2 tbsp parsley, chopped
1 tbsp olive oil

1 oz dulse, rinsed and chopped
2 sheets nori seaweed, toasted and
   crumbled
1 tbsp tamari

Bake the potatoes, then scrape the middles into a bowl and mash. Add all the remaining ingredients except 4 oz of the oats. Shape into cakes and press the remaining oats on to the cakes and bake on an oiled tray for 30 minutes, at 200-220°C (400-425°F, gas mark 6/7).

Puddings

While we don't want to encourage a 'pudding at every dinner' culture, or the 'you won't get any pudding if you don't eat your dinner' game—or the concept of puddings and sweet foods as treats—sometimes it is nice to have 'a little bit extra', especially where active, growing children are concerned. Maybe provide a pudding two or three times a week to add variety to your youngster's diet.

RICE PUDDING

1 pint soya milk
1 dessertspoon honey

2 oz short grain brown rice
1 piece lemon rind

Bring the milk to the boil and add remaining ingredients and simmer gently for 5 minutes. Pour into an oven-proof dish and bake at 180°C (350°F, gas mark 4) for 40 minutes.

OAT COCKTAIL

6 tbsp rolled oats
1 tsp tahini
1 tbsp lemon flesh and juice
8 oz soft seasonal fruit

4 fl oz soya milk
1 tsp honey
5 oz soya yoghurt

Soak the oats in the soya milk in the fridge overnight. Blend the tahini, honey, lemon flesh and juice together and stir into the oats with the yoghurt and chosen fruit.

MILLET PUDDING

2 oz millet flakes   1 pint soya milk
Simmer gently for 45 minutes.

Flavour with:
1/2 tsp molasses   1 oz sultanas
Add 15 minutes before the end.

3 tbsp prune purée   1/2 tsp ground ginger
Add 5 minutes before the end.

1 small chopped apple e.g. Cox's   2 fl oz apple juice
Add 15 minutes before end.

ORANGE-BANANA PUDDING

4 peeled bananas   2 tbsp honey
Juice & zest of 1 large orange   1/2 tsp cinnamon
Pinch nutmeg   3 oz desiccated coconut
Vegan spread (for greasing dish)

Slice the bananas in half lengthways and place in a greased oven-proof
dish. Trickle honey, orange juice and zest over the bananas and sprinkle
with the spices. Cover with the coconut and bake at 180°C (350°F gas
mark 4) for 15 minutes.

Finger Foods & Snacks

Encourage your baby to eat finger foods as soon as he can hold and chew, to develop his co-ordination, chewing ability and independence. As he gets older he may be happier to graze on smaller amounts of food scattered throughout the day rather than three large meals, so these finger foods and snacks are ideal. They're also handy when out and about, and for ensuring a steady supply of energy as your child becomes more mobile.

1. Fresh fruit of all sorts. Remove stones from plums, peaches and nectarines. Cut fruit into manageable pieces.

2. Dried fruit—long strips of mango and pear are especially good to chew on.

3. Fresh vegetables such as slices of carrot or cucumber, with or without a dip such as houmous or vegetable paté.

4. Almond, date & coconut cookies (see page 93).

5. Sprouted sunflower seed biscuits.

6. Popcorn.

7. Oatcakes, spread with seed or nut butter.

8. Rice cakes with or without topping, try mashed banana and sesame seeds.

9. Apricot bars (see page 91) or Banana and Sunflower flapjack (see page 90).

10. Toast with a 100% fruit spread (no added sugar), vegetable paté, nut or seed butter.

11. Roast vegetables cut into chunky chips—carrot, courgette, potato, sweet potato, parsnip and pumpkin (coat with olive oil before baking).

Savouries

Encourage your toddler to eat fresh vegetables at every lunch and dinner meal—whether as part of a salad or as an accompaniment to a cooked meal. All recipes serve four. Refer to page 106 for instructions on making your own stock.

PARSNIP SOUP WITH GINGER

1 onion
1 oz ginger, peeled & grated
1 pint vegetable stock

1 tbsp olive oil
2 parsnips, scrubbed and cubed

Soften the onion in the olive oil for a few minutes, stir in the ginger and cook for a further minute. Add the parsnips and stock and simmer gently for 35 minutes. Liquidise and serve with sesame griddle cakes (see recipe on page 97).

BROCCOLI & LENTIL SOUP

4 small heads of broccoli
2 tbsp olive oil
$^{1}/_{2}$ tsp coriander
1 pint stock (or possibly more)

1 onion, chopped
$^{1}/_{2}$ tsp cumin
4 oz red lentils
4 oz tofu

Steam the broccoli until tender. Cook the onion gently in the oil, add the spices, then the lentils and stock and simmer for 10 minutes. Blend the broccoli and tofu together with the cooked lentils and stock. Check the consistency, adding more stock if required.

MINESTRONE SOUP

2 fl oz olive oil
1 medium carrot, diced
6 oz potato, diced
9 oz plum tomatoes, chopped
Handful of basil, chopped
1 leek, diced
3 oz short grain brown rice

1 medium onion, diced
2 stalks celery, diced
1½ pints vegetable stock
15 oz cooked cannellini beans
Handful of parsley, chopped
1 courgette, diced

Heat the olive oil in a large pan and cook the onion, carrot and celery for 2 to 3 minutes, add the potato and cook for a few minutes more, stirring all the time. Add the stock, leek, courgette, brown rice and tomatoes and cook for 30 minutes. Add the beans, basil and parsley and cook for a further 10 minutes and serve.

COURGETTE & CARROT SOUP

1 medium courgette
1 tbsp olive oil

1 clove garlic, chopped
4 carrots

Gently cook the courgette and garlic in the olive oil. Liquidise and set aside to cool. Juice the carrots and add to the courgettes. Serve with dulse and vegetable scones (see recipe on page 96).

RAW HOUMOUS

1 lb sprouted chick peas
1 clove garlic
1 tsp vegetable bouillon powder

Juice and flesh of 2 lemons
4 tbsp tahini
Water to thin, if necessary

Put all the ingredients into a food processor and blend. Serve as a dip for crudités.

AVOCADO & ALFALFA DIP

1 avocado, peeled and stoned   1 large handful of alfalfa
Juice of 1 lemon   1 clove garlic, peeled
1 tbsp chopped flat leaf parsley

Blend all ingredients together in a food processor. Use the same day as
you make it.

LENTIL & SUN-DRIED TOMATO PATÉ

8 oz red lentils   1 pint of stock
1 tsp chopped chives   2 sun-dried tomatoes

Cook the lentils in the stock until tender and there is no liquid left.
Combine with the chives and tomatoes and blend until smooth, turn out
into a serving dish and when cold serve with fresh baked bread.

ROAST POLENTA

Olive oil   1 onion, chopped
1 clove garlic, chopped   1¹/₂ pints stock
9oz polenta   1oz sun-dried tomatoes, finely chopped

Gently cook the onion and garlic in the oil until soft but not coloured.
Add the stock and sun-dried tomato and bring to the boil. Slowly pour
in the polenta, beating well. Cool briefly, pour into a well oiled tin and
allow to cool. Turn out and cut into small shapes. Place on an oiled
baking sheet and roast in a hot oven until crisp (about 10 minutes).

TOFU KOFTAS

1 red pepper, grated
1 medium carrot, grated
3 cloves garlic, finely chopped
1 tsp vegetable bouillon powder
1/2 tsp ground cinnamon
1 tbsp fresh mint, chopped
2 tbsp wholemeal flour

1 medium courgette, grated
1 small onion, finely chopped
2 tbsp olive oil
1/2 tsp ground turmeric
1/2 tsp ground cumin
1 lb firm tofu
2 tbsp olive oil

Cook the vegetables in the olive oil with a little water (to avoid browning) until tender and all the moisture has evaporated. Add the spices and cook for a further minute. Mash the tofu and add with the flour to the vegetables. Mix well, then form into small balls. Place on an oiled baking sheet and bake for about 30 minutes until firm at 180°C (350°F, gas mark 4).

BEETROOT MASH

Eating beetroot raw allows the body to make best use of the vegetable's nutritional and medicinal properties, but this dish nevertheless uses cooked beetroot. It is a terrific colour—adults and children will love it.

1 lb small beetroot
1 lb floury potatoes, peeled and cut into chunks

2 tbsp olive oil

Scrub the beetroot well and place in an ovenproof pan which has a tight fitting lid. Drizzle olive oil over them and roast for 1 1/2 hours at 160°C (325°F, gas mark 3). Slip the skins off the beetroot and cut into chunks. Put into a food processor and process to a purée. Put the potatoes into a large saucepan of boiling water and simmer for about 15 minutes or until tender. Drain. Return the potatoes to the saucepan and dry them out over a low heat shaking the pan gently. Mash the potatoes with 2 tablespoons of olive oil then mix in the beetroot purée. Serve with wholemeal pitta bread.

NETTLE MASH

Wild nettles are rich in minerals including iron and calcium, and are very high in chlorophyll.

2 lb floury potatoes, peeled & chopped
Large handful of freshly gathered nettles
4 tbsp olive oil

Using gloves, strip the leaves from the stems of the nettles. Soften in a little water. Tip the softened leaves and cooking liquid into a food processor along with the olive oil, and process to a purée. Cook the potatoes in boiling water for 15 minutes or until tender. Drain. Return to the pan and stir, gently drying out the potatoes. Remove from the heat and mash with the nettle mixture. Makes an excellent dip with chunks of carrot, celery, cucumber and broccoli.

GARLIC MASH

Garlic is extremely good for you. It is a natural antibiotic and stimulates the activity of all digestive organs. It is rich in calcium, sulphur, zinc, copper and potassium.

2 lb floury potatoes, peeled & chopped
2 cloves garlic, peeled and crushed into 4 tablespoons olive oil
4 tbsp chopped parsley

Cook the potatoes in boiling water for 15 minutes or until tender. Drain and return to the pan, gently dry out the potatoes before mashing with the garlic oil. When well mashed and fluffy, stir in the chopped parsley and serve.

BROCCOLI WITH SESAME, GINGER AND CORIANDER

Chunk of grated ginger
Small bunch coriander, chopped

5 tablespoons sesame oil
1^1/$_2$ lb broccoli

Mix the ginger, sesame oil and coriander together. Steam the broccoli for 1–2 minutes. Cool, then toss in the dressing.

HEMP ROAST

1 onion
4 tbsp olive oil
1 tsp ground ginger
4 oz chopped courgettes
3 oz ground hemp seeds
4 oz chopped nuts
2 oz tomato purée

2 cloves garlic
^{1}/$_2$ tsp turmeric, cumin, chilli
4 oz grated carrot
4 oz chopped mushrooms
2 oz oatmeal
2 oz coconut

Mix all the ingredients together into a thick paste—you could also add an egg if you want. Grease a 1 lb loaf tin and bake for 30–40 minutes at 180°C (350°F, gas mark 4).

SAMOSAS

Pastry

8 oz wholewheat flour   4 tbsp oil
4 tbsp water

Mix oil with the flour until it resembles coarse breadcrumbs, then gradually add water to make a stiff dough. Knead for 3–4 minutes, place in an oiled basin, cover and leave to rest.

Filling

1 tsp olive oil   1 small onion, finely chopped
$1/2$ tsp turmeric $1/2$ tsp ground cumin
$1/2$ tsp ground coriander $1/2$ tsp seed mustard
$1/2$ tsp grated root ginger   1 clove garlic, peeled & crushed
8 oz cooked diced potatoes   4 oz sprouted mung beans
Juice of $1/2$ lemon

Cook the onion in the oil until soft. Add all the spices and cook for a further 30 seconds. Add the potatoes and toss well. Add the sprouted mung beans and lemon juice. Roll out the pastry and cut into 4" disks. Spread the filling on half of each disk leaving a margin around the edge. Moisten this margin with water and fold the other half of the dough over the filling so that the edges meet, making a half moon turnover. Press the edges firmly together by twisting and pinching. Put on to an oiled baking tray and brush with soya milk and bake for 20 minutes at 190°C (375°F, gas mark 5).

AUBERGINE, COURGETTE & TOMATO PIZZA

Base:

2 oz strong white unbleached 'O' grade pizza flour *(Doves)*
1/2 oz fresh yeast
Pinch of sugar
2 fl oz olive oil

6 oz wholemeal flour
1/2 tsp sea salt (optional)
2 fl oz warm water
1/2 tsp sea salt (optional)

Sieve the flour and salt into a bowl and make a well. Into this add the yeast, warm water and pinch of sugar, cover with a little flour and leave in a warm place for 10 minutes. Adding the oil, mix the liquid into the flour to make a soft, pliable dough. Turn out on to a floured board and knead for 15 minutes. Place the dough in a clean lightly oiled bowl, cover with a clean tea towel and leave in a warm place for an hour, or until doubled in size. Meanwhile prepare the topping (see below).

Turn the dough on to a floured surface and roll out very thinly producing a 12" thick round base. Cover thickly with the topping, place on a hot baking sheet and bake in a preheated oven, 200°C (400°C, gas mark 6) for 20 minutes until golden and crisp.

Topping:

1 aubergine
6 tomatoes
6 basil leaves
Olive oil

2 courgettes
2 cloves garlic
1 tsp tomato purée

Dice the aubergines into 1 cm cubes, place on a baking tray then gently by hand coat with 2 tablespoons of olive oil. Dice the courgettes into about 1 cm cubes, place on a baking tray and treat in the same way. Put both trays in a hot oven and roast until the vegetables start to turn golden brown (about 10 minutes). While the aubergine and courgette are roasting, skin the tomatoes by placing in boiling water for 30 seconds and then plunging into cold—the skins will then peel off. Cut into quarters and remove the seeds. Dice the tomato flesh, peel and chop the garlic and mix together with the tomato purée and the shredded basil. When the aubergine and courgette is ready, add to the tomato mixture and stir well.

PENNE WITH BROAD BEANS & PEAS

8 oz wholemeal penne
6 oz shelled peas
1 garlic clove, crushed
6 leaves of mint, chopped

6 oz shelled broad beans
1 tbsp olive oil
1 onion, chopped
1 tbsp chopped parsley

Cook the penne in a large saucepan of boiling salted water for 10 minutes. Steam the broad beans and peas for about 5 minutes. Gently cook the onion and garlic in the olive oil. Drain the pasta and mix in the onion and garlic, broad beans and peas, and mint and parsley. Toss well together and serve.

TOFU NUT PATTIES

3 oz short grain rice
1 tbsp soy sauce
2 oz ground hazelnuts
4 oz wholemeal breadcrumbs

1/2 lb firm tofu
2 oz ground almonds
1 tsp grated ginger

Simmer the rice until 'mushy'. Blend with the tofu and then mix in the remaining ingredients. Shape into little patties. Bake on a greased baking tray at 180°C (350°F, gas mark 4) for 20 minutes.

WHOLEMEAL SPAGHETTI WITH TOMATO, OLIVE & BASIL SAUCE

2 tbsp olive oil
1 onion, peeled & chopped
1 oz basil leaves & stalks coarsely chopped
1 lb tomatoes, quartered
4 oz black olives, stoned & chopped
10 oz wholemeal spaghetti

1 garlic clove, peeled & crushed
8 basil leaves, finely shredded

2 tbsp tomato purée

First make the sauce: Gently cook the onion and garlic in the olive oil. Then after a few minutes add the basil and cook for a further few seconds. Add the tomatoes and tomato purée and simmer for 10 minutes. Cool slightly and press through a sieve. Return to the pan, add the olives and basil, and keep warm. Cook the spaghetti in a large pan of boiling salted water for about 10 minutes or until just tender. Drain the pasta and toss with the sauce.

BROWN RICE WITH BROCCOLI & TOFU

3–4 tbsp soy sauce
2 tsp grated ginger
1/2 lb firm tofu
1 head broccoli, cut into small florets

2 cloves garlic, peeled & crushed
2 tbsp olive oil
6 oz brown rice

Combine the soya sauce, garlic, ginger and olive oil. Add the tofu (diced) and leave covered for at least 1 hour, preferably overnight. Cook the rice. Steam the broccoli for 5 minutes. Combine the tofu and its marinade with the rice and broccoli and serve.

ROOT VEGETABLES
WITH CORNMEAL CRUST

Vegetables:

1 small turnip

1 sweet potato

Juice of ¹/₂ lemon in 1 pint water

2 carrots, scrubbed

2 red onions

¹/₂ tsp chopped rosemary

1 tsp tomato purée

1 pint stock

1 parsnip

1 small celeriac

2 leeks

1 small fennel bulb

1 tsp chopped thyme

1 tbsp chopped parsley

2 cloves garlic, chopped

Peel the turnip and slice into pieces about ¹/₂" thick, then slice these into strips. Treat the parsnip, sweet potato, and celeriac root in the same way (peel the celeriac root first, and drop the strips into the lemon water to prevent discolouring). Finely slice the leeks, onions, carrots and fennel. Strain the celeriac into a stainless steel pan. Add the other vegetables, herbs, tomato purée, garlic and stock, cover and simmer gently for 15 minutes. Remove the cover and reduce the liquid until you have a thick vegetable mixture. Pour into an ovenproof dish.

Cornmeal Crust:

1¹/₂ pints vegetable stock   6 oz quick cook polenta

In a large saucepan bring the stock to the boil. Gradually pour in the polenta stirring constantly to prevent lumps forming. Simmer gently for a few minutes with the lid on as it is inclined to bubble and spit. Remove from the heat and pour over the vegetables. Smooth over, sprinkle with olive oil and bake for 20 minutes 180°C (350°F, gas mark 4) until golden.

PANCAKES

6 oz wholemeal flour
2 tbsp olive oil

$^1/_2$ pint soya milk

Beat together the wholemeal flour, the milk and olive oil, then chill for 30 minutes.

Reserving a pan specifically for pancakes will ensure it is so well conditioned that you don't need to add oil, except a little wiped round with a kitchen towel.

Heat the pan, pour in sufficient batter to make a thin 'cake', swirl it round to reach the sides and cook for 1 minute or until set, flip it over and cook the other side. Continue with the remaining mixture.

PANCAKE FILLINGS

Tofu & vegetable

3 oz tofu
6 basil leaves
8 oz finely diced mixture of vegetables,
    e.g. carrot, fennel, mange tout, celery

1 tsp mustard seeds
A little stock

Blend the tofu, mustard seeds, and sufficient vegetable stock to form a creamy consistency. Stir in the vegetables, and fill your pancake!

Mashed Avocado with Diced Red Pepper & Chopped Watercress

1 ripe avocado
$^1/_2$ bunch watercress with stalks removed & leaves finely chopped

$^1/_2$ red pepper, finely diced

Cut the avocado in half, remove the stone and scoop out the flesh into a bowl. Mash the avocado with a fork and stir in the red pepper and watercress.

Wilted Curly Kale with Garlic & Chives

1 tbsp olive oil	1 lb shredded curly kale
2 cloves garlic, crushed	1 tbsp chives, finely chopped

Stir fry the kale and garlic in a wok with 1 tablespoonful of olive oil and 1 dessertspoonful of water. When it is wilted, stir in the chives and serve.

BLINIS WITH TAPENADE

½ oz fresh yeast	Pinch sugar
12 oz lukewarm soya milk	4 oz wholemeal flour
5 oz buckwheat flour	2 tbsp olive oil

Cream the yeast and sugar with a little soya milk. Gradually add the remaining soya milk and beat in the wholemeal flour. Leave in a warm place to prove for 45 minutes. Beat in the buckwheat flour and olive oil. Heat a frying pan and very lightly oil the bottom. Cooking three or four blinis at a time, for each drop a tablespoon of the batter into the pan, heat until bubbles start to appear and the edges are set (2–3 minutes), turn and cook the other side until browned (about 2 minutes). Store on a plate in a warm oven until the remainder are cooked.

To serve:
Spread a little tapenade (see below) on each blini and serve, or try raw houmous (see page 65).

TAPENADE

4 tbsp olive oil	1 large peeled clove garlic
Juice of a small lemon	9 oz pitted and oil-cured black olives

Combine all ingredients in a blender until smooth.

STUFFED GRIDDLE BREADS

4 oz buckwheat flour
Pinch salt (optional)
Approximately 6 fl oz water

4 oz wholemeal flour
2 tbsp olive oil

Combine the flour and salt in a bowl, making a well in the centre. Pour in the olive oil and half the water. Slowly incorporate the flour, adding more water until you have a supple and elastic dough (the exact quantity of water will vary according to the flour). Knead the dough well for 5 minutes, cover and leave to prove for 30 minutes. If the dough is kept for a longer time, e.g. overnight, store in a cool place. Form the dough into small round balls and flatten them with the palm of your hand. Dust with flour, then roll out thinly. Heat and very lightly oil a griddle (or frying pan if you do not have a griddle). Cook the bread until the first bubbles rise (about 3 minutes). Turn over and cook for a further 3 minutes. Stack the breads on a plate and cover with a cloth.

To serve, roll up with any of the following.

1. Vegetable paté (page 81)
2. Sunny vegetable burgers (page 78)
3. Gazpacho salad (see page 78)
4. Mashed avocado & alfalfa sprouts
5. Mashed avocado, finely chopped spinach & diced red pepper
6. Mashed tofu with grated carrot, cabbage, spring onions, ginger, garlic and miso
7. Mashed avocado with dulse flakes & sprouted lentils
8. Houmous with pitted olives
9. Broccoli with sesame, ginger & coriander (see page 69)
10. Tofu koftas & alfalfa sprouts (see page 67)

GAZPACHO SALAD

2 ripe avocados
1 red pepper
1/2 cucumber
2 skinned & seeded tomatoes
1 tbsp chopped coriander

Juice of 1 small lime
1 yellow pepper
1 small red onion
1 tbsp chopped parsley
1 tbsp of olive oil

Peel, stone and dice the avocado, place in a bowl and pour over the lime juice. Dice the peppers, cucumber, onion and tomatoes, and add to the avocado mixture with the herbs and the oil. Serve by itself or as a filling for pitta or griddle bread. Small hands may find it easier to manage if you lightly mash the mixture together.

SUNNY VEGETABLE BURGERS

3 tbsp flax seed
8 oz carrot pulp (from juicer)
6 spring onions, finely diced
1 red pepper, very finely diced
1 clove garlic, finely diced

6 tbsp carrot juice
4 sticks celery, finely diced
2 tbsp parsley, finely chopped
1 tbsp dulse, finely chopped
6 oz sunflower seeds, ground

Grind the flax seeds in a coffee grinder, mix in the carrot juice and pour into a bowl, adding the carrot pulp, celery, onions, parsley, red peppers, dulse, garlic and sunflower seeds. Mix thoroughly and shape into six burgers. Serve them as they are, or if you prefer them warm, heat through in a moderate oven, 180°C (350°F, gas mark 4) for 15 minutes. Delicious with red pepper sauce.

Red Pepper Sauce

2 medium red peppers
2 tbsp coriander
1 clove garlic, peeled

2 tbsp parsley
1 tsp bouillon powder
A little water

Mix all the ingredients together in a food processor, adding a little water to make a thick sauce.

MARINADED MUSHROOMS

1 pound medium mushrooms, cleaned & trimmed but left whole
3 oz olive oil   Juice & zest of 1 lemon
2 cloves garlic, crushed   1 teaspoon sea salt (optional)

Put the mushrooms in a bowl. Whisk together the olive oil, lemon juice, zest, garlic and salt and pour over the mushrooms, leave to marinade up to 2 hours at room temperature or overnight in the fridge, bring to room temperature before serving.

These are also delicious stuffed with tapenade recipe on page 77.

CUCUMBER, CARROT, AVOCADO & MINT SALAD

1 cucumber   2 medium carrots
2 avocado   8 mint leaves, finely shredded
1 dessertspoon olive oil   1 teaspoon lemon juice
4 sprigs parsley

Mix the mint, olive oil and lemon juice together in a bowl. Carefully cut the avocado in half, remove the stone and discard. Keep the empty shells. Scoop out the flesh, cut into small dice and add to the dressing in the bowl. Grate the cucumber and carrots and add to the avocado mixture. Mix well. Fill the empty avocado shells with this mixture, decorate with sprigs of parsley and serve.

CAULIFLOWER, TOMATO & BASIL SALAD

1 cauliflower cut into florets
10 basil leaves shredded

6 tomatoes, skinned, seeded
& diced

Put the cauliflower in a bowl and stir in the remaining ingredients. Leave for a couple of hours at room temperature so the flavours can develop.

To skin a tomato, put into boiling water for 30 seconds then immediately plunge into cold, drain and skin.

TAHINI DRESSING

Juice ½ lemon
2 tbsp tahini

Pinch of cumin & paprika
4 fl oz water

Combine the lemon juice, cumin, paprika and tahini in the blender. Add the water a little at a time to get the consistency you want. Pour over salads or raw vegetables.

SESAME GARLIC DRESSING

2 tbsp tahini
2 cloves garlic

4 fl oz water
2 tsp toasted sesame seeds

Combine the garlic, sesame seeds and tahini in the blender. Add the water a little at a time to the required consistency. Pour over salads or raw vegetables.

VEGETABLE PATÉ

4 carrots
1 stick celery
1 clove garlic, peeled
2 tbsp flax seed
6 pitted olives

1 red onion
1 red pepper
1 small head broccoli
4 oz sprouted mung beans
2 tsp Udo's oil

Using a heavy duty juicer with a blank screen, juice the carrots, onion, celery, pepper, garlic and broccoli into a bowl. Grind the flax seeds and blend with the Udo's oil and remaining mung beans and olives, ensuring the mixture maintains texture. Add the other vegetables and blend. Turn into a clean bowl and chill for at least an hour. Delicious stuffed in pitta bread (see page 94).

WOK GREENS WITH TOFU

4 oz tofu cut into cubes
2 cloves garlic, sliced
1½ lb shredded greens (e.g. spinach, beet tops, chard, mustard greens, bokchoy)

1 tbsp Soya sauce
2 tsp olive oil

Marinade the tofu in the soya sauce and garlic overnight or for at least 2 hours. Then stir fry the garlic in the olive oil. Add the greens and stir until wilted. Mix in the tofu with its marinade and serve.

These green tops are especially good for you, and as most youngsters will not eat a plate of raw greens this is a very good alternative. Quickly cooking the greens preserves a fair amount of nutrients.

FALAFEL

1 lb chickpeas, soaked overnight   2 pints vegetable stock
2 tbsp olive oil   3 cloves garlic, finely chopped
1 onion, finely chopped   1 tsp ground coriander
1 tsp ground cumin   2 tbsp tahini
2 tbsp fresh parsley   2 tbsp fresh coriander

Cook the chickpeas in vegetable stock until tender (1½ hours). Meanwhile soften the garlic and onion in the olive oil, and add the coriander and cumin powder. Stir in the tahini and fresh herbs.

Drain the chickpeas (saving the liquid) and mash in a bowl or blender, then mix in the garlic mixture. If the mixture is too stiff, add a little of the chickpea stock. Form the mixture into small round patties, place on an oiled baking tray and bake for 15 minutes 180°C, (350°F, gas mark 4). Serve with tahini dressing (see page 80).

Puddings

RASPBERRY CRUMBLE

1 lb raspberries
4 oz vegan spread
2 oz rolled oats
1 tsp ground ginger

2 tbsp honey
4 oz wholewheat flour
1 oz desiccated coconut

Place the raspberries in the bottom of an ovenproof dish and drizzle the honey over them. Rub the spread into the flour, then mix in the oats, coconut and ginger. Place over the raspberries and bake for 30 minutes at 190°C (375°F, gas mark 5).

FRUITY RICE PUDDING

2 pints soya milk
2 tbsp honey
$^1/_2$ tsp vanilla essence
$^1/_2$ tsp cinnamon
$4^1/_2$ oz ground almonds

$2^1/_2$ oz pudding rice
8 finely sliced apricots soaked in
  orange water
2 oz raisins
2 tbsp ground rice

Bring the milk to the boil, add the pudding rice and simmer very gently for $^1/_2$ hour. Add the honey, apricots, vanilla essence, cinnamon and raisins and simmer for another $^1/_2$ hour. Stir in the ground rice and ground almonds, adding more milk if required. Heat through for 10 more minutes, then serve. This is also delicious cold.

ALMOND/SEMOLINA CAKE
WITH RASPBERRY SAUCE

4 oz vegan spread
1 dessertspoon lemon juice
10 fl oz soya yogurt
12 oz semolina
1 tsp baking powder

Flesh of 1 lemon
5 oz sugar
4 oz ground almonds
1 tsp bicarbonate of soda

Combine the spread, lemon flesh and juice with the sugar, yoghurt and ground almonds. Blend to a creamy constituency. Then add the remaining ingredients and blend until smooth (about 30 seconds in a processor). Pour into a 9" lined cake tin and bake for 25 minutes at 150°C (300°F, gas mark 2). Turn out, and serve warm or cold with raspberry sauce (blending and sieving 1 lb fresh raspberries). Decorate with lemon balm.

BAKED BANANAS

4 firm bananas, unpeeled
Zest & juice of ½ orange

3 oz raspberries
2 tsp honey

Place the bananas on a baking tray and bake for 15 minutes at 200°C (400°F, gas mark 6). Sieve the raspberries and mix with the honey. Snip open the bananas, sprinkle on the orange zest and juice, and then drizzle the raspberry sauce into the opening.

COCONUT CREAM

1/2 lb creamed coconut
3 tbsp soya milk

1/2 pint water
Juice 1/2 lemon

Coarsely chop the coconut cream and stir into the water, creating a smooth cream. Blend the soya milk, coconut cream mixture and lemon until smooth and thick.

CASHEW CREAM

6 oz cashews

1/2 pint apple juice or rice milk

Blend the cashews and liquid until thick and creamy (juicers such as 'The Champion' have a homogenising function which is ideal for this recipe). Two teaspoonsful of Udo's Choice can be added as desired.

DOUBLE CREAM

1 vanilla pod
4 oz tofu
2 tbsp maple syrup

6 tbsp soya milk
4 tbsp sunflower oil

Split open the vanilla pod and leave to infuse into the soya milk. Scrape the seeds into the milk and dispose of the pod, and blend all ingredients together until thick and creamy.

ALMOND MILK

6 oz blanched almonds   1 pint spring water

Grind the almonds. Add the water and blend until the mixture is smooth. Either strain, or use as it is. Thicken the mixture by reducing the amount of liquid, and sweeten if desired with maple syrup. Alternatively, a similar but blander milk can be made using cashew nuts, or pine kernels can be used to make a much richer milk.

NUT BUTTERS

These are simple if you can homogenise with a juicer such as The Champion (see juicers on page 110).

Assemble the juicer for homogenising, feed the nuts slowly into the machine, adding a little olive oil if the mixture is too dry. The best nut butters are almond and cashew. If you don't have a suitable juicer for making nut butters, try using a food processor.

TRUFFLES

4 oz hazelnuts   4 oz walnuts
6 oz raisins   6 oz apricots
1 oz carob powder

Soak all the ingredients overnight in a little water, and then blend well. Roll into small balls and coat in carob powder to make small truffles.

ALMOND HALVAH

12 oz almonds
6 level tsp set honey

6 good tsp tahini
1 tsp vanilla

Finely grind the almonds. Mix thoroughly with the tahini, honey and vanilla. Roll into a ball and refrigerate for 30 minutes. Cut into bite-size pieces and form into small balls. Serve as they are, or rolled in carob powder, sesame seeds or desiccated coconut.

BANANA ICE

If you have a heavy-duty juicer you can make delicious ices. Keep a bag of frozen bananas in the fridge and you can treat your children at any time to sugar-free, fat-free, cholesterol-free, delicious yet simple banana ice cream. Using the blank screen on your juicer, push through 1 or 2 bananas, catching the result in a cup, and serve at once. Banana ice is a firm favourite with our children. Also delicious with a few frozen raspberries scattered on top, or carob sauce.

SWEET PANCAKES

Add fruit fillings such as mashed banana and maple syrup or blended kiwifruit and raspberry to the pancake recipe on page 75.

Cakes, Bars & Little Extras

DATE CAKE

¹/₂ lb dates
3 oz vegan spread
¹/₂ tsp cinnamon
8 oz wholewheat flour
1 tsp bicarbonate of soda

¹/₂ pint soya milk
4 oz sultanas
¹/₂ tsp nutmeg
1 tsp baking powder

Chop the dates and boil in the soya milk until mushy. Add the spread and sultanas, boiling for a further few minutes. Remove and add the remaining ingredients. Mix and bake for 30 minutes at 190°C (375°F, gas mark 5).

WALNUT & APRICOT SQUARES

5 oz dried apricots, sliced
8 oz walnuts
4 oz vegan spread
1¹/₂ tsp baking powder

¹/₂ pint soya milk
2 oz brown sugar
4 oz wholewheat flour
2 oz brown sugar

Soak the apricots in the soya milk for at least 2 hours. Blend the walnuts and sugar until fine. Gently incorporate the apricot mixture and vegan spread (pulse for about 30 seconds). Fold in the flour and baking powder (or pulse together for 30 seconds). Turn into a 7" square tin lined with parchment paper. Bake for 25 minutes at 160°C (325°F, gas mark 3), turn out, cool and cut into squares.

SESAME SQUARES

3 oz vegan spread
6 tsp honey
2 oz desiccated coconut

6 tsp tahini
4 oz sesame seeds
8 oz rolled oats

Beat the vegan spread, tahini and honey until smooth (about 45 seconds in a processor). Add the sesame seeds, blending well (pulse for a further 30 seconds). Mix in the coconut and oats, and turn into a 9" square lined tin. Firm down well and bake at 160°C (325°F, gas mark 3) for 20 minutes, taking care not to burn.

BANANA LOAF

2 large bananas
4 fl oz soya milk
6 oz wholemeal flour
1 tsp baking powder
4 oz sultanas

2 oz vegan spread
2 oz brown sugar
2 oz ground almonds
2 tsp cinnamon

Chop the banana and blend with the vegan spread, soya milk and sugar for 30 seconds or until well mixed. Combine the flour, almonds, baking powder, cinnamon and sultanas. Blend the two mixtures and transfer into a prepared tin. Bake in a pre-heated oven at 180°C (350°F, gas mark 4) for 50 minutes or until golden and cooked through. Cool in the tin for 10 minutes. Serve in slices.

BANANA & SUNFLOWER FLAPJACK

4 oz vegan spread
13 oz porridge
2 oz ground sunflower seeds
1 oz sultanas

3 tbsp honey
$^1/_2$ tsp baking powder
2 ripe mashed bananas

Preheat oven to 170°C (345°F, gas mark 4$^1/_2$). Lightly grease and line a 8" x 8" tin with parchment paper. Melt the spread and honey in a pan and stir in the remaining ingredients. Spread the mixture out in the tin and bake for 15–20 minutes until very light golden. Cool slightly, and turn out on a board. Cut into squares whilst still warm.

GINGERBREAD

9 oz wholewheat flour
1 tsp baking powder
3 tsp ground ginger
4$^1/_2$ oz vegan spread
6 fl oz soya milk

1 level tsp bicarbonate of soda
1 tsp mixed spice
2 oz sultanas
4$^1/_2$ oz molasses

Grease and line a loaf tin. Combine the flour, bicarbonate of soda, baking powder, mixed spice, ground ginger and sultanas. Gently melt together the vegan spread and molasses. Fold into the dry ingredients with the soya milk and mix well. Pour into the prepared tin and bake at 180°C (350°F, gas mark 4) for approximately 45 minutes. Turn out and cool.

POPCORN

1 tbsp of olive oil   3 tbsp of popcorn kernels
1 tbsp of roasted sesame seeds

Heat the oil in a deep, heavy bottomed pan. Add the kernels, shake the
pan and cover with a lid. Leave over a fairly high heat, and after shaking
from time to time you will begin to hear the popcorn pop. Do not take
the lid off until the popping stops. When popping has ceased, turn into
a dish and scatter over with sesame seeds.

APRICOT BARS

6 oz vegan spread   2 tbsp honey
3 oz finely chopped apricots $7^1/_2$ oz self-raising flour
1 oz desiccated coconut   3 oz soya yogurt
2 oz sultanas

Warm (melt) the spread with the honey and chopped apricots and then
remove from the heat. Cool slightly, then stir in the remaining
ingredients. Bake at 180°C (350°F, gas mark 4) for 15 minutes in a
prepared 8" tin. Turn out, cool and cut into fingers.

Dehydration

Dehydration is the simplest, most natural and oldest method used to preserve food. A dehydrator is not the most important piece of equipment to buy, but if you do have one it will give you the opportunity to preserve fruits and vegetables when you have too many to eat straight away, and it will expand your repertoire of delicious recipes. Dehydrators are used to dry food while leaving the enzymes intact (see page 16). Here are a few of our favourite dehydrator recipes.

1. SPROUTED SUNFLOWER CRACKERS

2 handfuls of sprouted sunflower seeds (about 2 days growth)
1 tbsp raisins

Grind the sprouts with the raisins until the mixture forms a ball. Roll this out to a thin sheet on a lightly floured board. Using a 1¹/₂" diameter cutter, cut out and place on dehydrator tray. Dehydrate for about 4–6 hours (this can also be done on a radiator top, in an airing cupboard or on a sunny windowsill).

2. PARSNIP CRISPS

Scrub 3 large parsnips and cut into thin disks. Place on the dehydrator tray and dehydrate for about 6 hours, turning once. Store in a sealed container.

3. MANGO STRIPS

Peel two ripe mangos and cut the flesh lengthways off the stone. Cut into even long strips. Place on a dehydrator tray lined with parchment paper. When half-dry remove paper, turnover and dry for a further 2 hours. These make delicious snack food when out and about.

4. ALMOND, DATE & COCONUT COOKIES

12 oz almonds   6 oz stoned dates
2 oz shredded coconut

Soak the almonds overnight in water, drain and rinse. Blend all the ingredients until a ball is formed. Shape into small cookies. Place on the dehydrator tray and dehydrate for approximately 6 hours.

Breads, Muffins & Scones

PITTA BREAD

1 lb wholemeal flour *(Doves)*	$1/2$ tsp salt (optional)
$1/2$ oz fresh yeast	Pinch of sugar
$1/2$ pint tepid water	3 tbsp olive oil

Sift the flour and salt into a bowl. Make a well in the centre and add the yeast, pinch of sugar and 6 tablespoons of the tepid water. Cover the liquid with some of the flour, and leave until it begins to froth. Then mix with 2 tablespoons of the olive oil and enough of the remaining water to make a firm but not too hard dough. Knead the dough well for about 10 minutes until it is smooth and elastic and no longer sticks to your fingers. Coat the inside of a clean bowl with olive oil, put in the dough, and roll around to grease the dough surface. Cover the bowl with a dampened cloth and leave in a warm place until the dough has doubled in size (about $1^1/2 - 2$ hours).

Turn the dough on to a floured board and divide into six. Flatten each piece with a floured rolling pin, forming into $1/2$" thick ovals. Place these on a floured cloth in a warm place. Cover with another cloth and leave to rise for 20 minutes.

Preheat your oven to the highest setting and pop in two lightly oiled baking sheets. When the pittas have risen, slip them carefully on to the baking sheets, splash with water and bake for 10 minutes without opening the door. Cool on a rack.

BUCKWHEAT FLATBREAD

1 lb buckwheat flour
1/2 tsp salt (optional)
1 tsp sugar
8 oz olive oil

8 oz wholemeal flour
2 oz fresh yeast
16 fl oz tepid water

Combine the flours and salt into a bowl, making a well in the centre. Into this add the yeast, sugar and 4 fl oz water. Leave in a warm place until frothy. Add the olive oil and enough water to make a pliable dough. Turn out on to a floured board and knead well until it is no longer sticky. Place in an oiled basin, cover with a damp cloth and leave in a warm place for an hour. Turn out and gently knead and shape into a large flat circle, place on a 10" pie tin and prove for 30 minutes. Preheat oven to 180°C (350°F, gas mark 4) and bake for 30 minutes.

RYE BREAD

1 1/2 lb coarse rye flour
1/2 tsp salt (optional)
1 tsp sugar
8 fl oz molasses

12 oz strong plain wholemeal flour
2 oz fresh yeast
1 1/2 pints soya milk
2 tbsp fennel seeds

Combine the flours and the salt in a bowl, making a well in the centre. Into this add the yeast, sugar and 1/2 pint soya milk. Leave in a warm place until liquid is frothy. Add the molasses, fennel seeds and enough of the remaining soya milk to make a pliable dough, and turn on to a floured board. Knead well until no longer sticky. Place in a clean bowl, cover and leave in a warm place for 1 1/2 hours. Turn out and knead lightly before shaping into loaves and putting into oiled tins. Bake at 190°C (375°F, gas mark 5) for about 1/2 hour depending on the size of the loaf.

MIXED SEED AND GRAIN BREAD

2½ lb wholemeal flour | 4 oz buckwheat flour
4 oz oats | 1 tsp salt (optional)
1 oz fresh yeast | 1 tsp sugar
½–1 pint soya milk | 2 tbsp sesame seeds
2 tbsp sunflower seeds, ground | 2 tbsp pumpkin seeds, ground

Combine the flours, oats and salt in a bowl, making a well in the centre. Into this pour the yeast, sugar and 4 fl oz tepid water and leave for 15 minutes. Add the remaining ingredients with enough soya milk to make a stiff, sticky dough. Turn on to a floured board and knead until smooth. Shape into a ball and leave covered in an oiled bowl until double in size. Turn out on to a floured board and knead into loaves or rolls. Bake at 200°C (400°F, gas mark 6) for 20 minutes (rolls), or 35 minutes (loaves).

DULSE & VEGETABLE SCONES

12 oz self raising wholemeal flour | 1 tsp baking powder
1 oz vegan spread | 1 dessertspoon chopped dulse
2 oz butternut squash, grated | 2 oz courgette, grated
½ pint soya milk

Sieve the flour and baking powder into a bowl. Rub in the spread, and stir in the dulse, squash and courgette and enough milk to make a manageable dough. Roll out and cut into rounds. Place on an oiled baking tray and bake for 12–15 minutes at 180°C (350°F, gas mark 4).

SESAME GRIDDLE CAKES

12 oz wholemeal flour
1/2 tsp salt (optional)
2 oz sesame seeds

1 tsp baking powder
2 oz vegan spread
8 oz soya milk

Lightly oil and heat a heavy based frying pan. Sieve together the flour, baking powder and salt and rub in the vegan spread (to form a breadcrumb-like consistency). Stir in the sesame seeds, and then mix in the soya milk to make a soft but manageable dough. Turn the dough on to a floured surface and roll into a large circle. Cut into 6 and place the pieces on to the griddle. Cook over a low heat for about 5 minutes then turn the cakes carefully with a palette knife and cook until golden.

LEEK, RED PEPPER, ONION & BLACK OLIVE SCONES

2 tbsp olive oil
2 oz diced red peppers
1 tbsp chopped parsley
8 pitted black olives, chopped
5 oz wholewheat flour
6 fl oz soya milk

4 oz chopped onions
2 oz leek, sliced into rings
1 tbsp chopped thyme
5 oz rye flour
2 tbsp baking powder

Gently cook the vegetables in the olive oil for a few minutes, then stir in the parsley, thyme and black olives. Combine the flours and the baking powder in a mixing bowl and stir in the vegetables and soya milk to make a medium soft dough. Turn out on to a floured board and roll to approximately 1/2 inch thick. Cut with a 11/2" diameter cutter and place on a baking sheet. Bake for 15 minutes in a moderate oven (200°C/400°F, gas mark 6).

FRUIT MUFFINS

8 oz wholewheat flour
2 tsp baking powder
2 oz coconut
2 oz finely chopped apricots
1 mashed banana
1 tbsp olive oil

2 oz medium polenta
1 tsp bicarbonate of soda
2 oz raisins
1 apple, grated
$^1/_2$ pint soya yogurt
A little soya milk

Combine the flour, polenta, baking powder and bicarbonate of soda. Add the coconut, raisins, apricots, and apple and mix well. Mix together the banana, yogurt and olive oil and add to the dry ingredients (add soya milk as required to make a soft dropping consistency). Pour into 12 muffin cases and bake for 15 minutes in a moderate oven (200°C/400°F, gas mark 6).

PUMPKIN, GINGER & SESAME MUFFINS

12 oz wholewheat flour
Pinch salt (optional)
3 tbsp vegan spread
1 tbsp sesame seeds
A little soya milk

3 tsp baking powder
1 dessertspoon grated ginger
1 tbsp sugar
8 oz steamed and mashed pumpkin

Combine the flour, salt, baking powder and ginger in a bowl and rub in the spread. Stir in the sugar and sesame seeds, add the pumpkin and enough soya milk to make a soft dropping consistency. Pour into 10 muffin cases and bake for 15 minutes in a moderate oven (200°C/400°F, gas mark 6).

CARROT, CELERY, RAISIN & WALNUT MUFFINS

10 oz wholemeal flour
1 carrot
2 oz walnuts
2 oz sprouted wheat
2 oz olive oil

3 teaspoons baking powder
2 sticks celery from the middle
2 oz raisins
4 oz soya yogurt
A little soya milk

Combine the flour and baking powder in a bowl. Finely grate the carrot and finely dice the celery. Finely grind the walnuts. Mix the carrots, celery, walnuts, raisins and sprouted wheat with the other dry ingredients. Then add the soya yogurt and olive oil, and enough soya milk to make a soft dropping consistency. Pour into 10 muffin cases and bake for 15 minutes in a moderate oven (200°C/400°F, gas mark 6).

Travelling Foods

When you're out and about you can still offer your baby or toddler healthy foods. Use old ice cream containers or similar for storage.

1. Fresh fruit

2. Fresh vegetables

3. Oatcakes, rice cakes and pitta bread

4. Houmous, tapenade, and lentil & sun-dried tomato paté

5. Nut & seed butter, and 100% fruit spreads on bread or toast

6. Home-baked muffins, scones, flapjacks, bars, etc.

7. Dried fruits

8. Frozen icecubes of leftover meals in recycled glass jar—use the same day the cubes begin to thaw

9. Organic sugar-free cereals and soya or rice milk

10. Drinking water or juices.

Party Food

If you're throwing a party for your little one, or taking food along to someone else's party, there are plenty of ideas for suitably fun, tasty and healthy foods.

1. Fresh fruit juices

2. Crudités, rice crackers and dips

3. Garlic bread

4. Stuffed giant pasta shells with mushrooms & sweetcorn, or tomato & peas or broccoli & ground pinenuts

5. Roast polenta

6. Sandwiches filled with: houmous & watercress; peanut butter (smooth); or banana & sesame

7. Popcorn with tamari

8. Pancakes with apple purée & maple syrup

9. Jacket potato with baked beans

10. Pizza (for recipe see page 71). Double the quantity and make a large rectangular pizza to cut into fingers.

Celebration Cakes

EASTER CHOCOLATE CAKE

1 lb dates
8 oz dark chocolate *(Plamil)*
3 oz walnuts
1 tsp baking powder
1 tsp bicarbonate of soda

$^1/_2$ pint fresh orange juice & flesh
4 oz vegan spread
12 oz wholemeal flour

Grease and then line a 10" round tin with greaseproof paper. Cook the dates in a little water until very soft, add the orange juice and reduce slightly and cool. Carefully melt chocolate in a bowl over hot water. Beat the vegan spread into the date mixture, and stir in the chocolate. Stir in the walnuts and sieve the flour, baking powder and bicarbonate of soda. Turn into the prepared tin. Smooth the top and bake until firm to touch (for about 40 minutes at 160°C (350°F, gas mark 4), reducing the temperature if required). Turn out on to a wire rack to cool.

Chocolate topping:
4 oz dark chocolate *(Plamil)*
1 oz vegan spread

1 oz soya cream

Melt the chocolate, add soya cream and vegan spread, mix well and spread over the cake. Decorate with ribbon and spring flowers as desired.

CHRISTMAS CAKE

1 lb plain wholewheat flour
1/2 tsp cinnamon
4 oz ground almonds
6 oz lexia raisins
3 oz sultanas
Flesh & juice of 2 oranges
1 tsp bicarbonate of soda

1/2 tsp ginger
4 oz brown sugar
4 oz ground walnuts
3 oz glacé cherries
4 oz walnut oil
4 fl oz soya milk
2 tbsp lemon juice

Line and grease a 10" cake tin. Preheat oven to 160°C (325°F, gas mark 3). Combine the flour, spices, sugar, ground nuts and fruit. Add the walnut oil, and juice and flesh of the oranges. Mix well. Gently warm the milk, add the bicarbonate of soda, and stir into the fruit mixture with the lemon juice. Bake for about 1 1/2–2 hours or until it is firm to the touch. Remove from the oven, cool in the tin for 20 minutes, then remove and cool on a wire rack. Can be decorated with crystallised fruits, bay leaves and ribbon.

BIRTHDAY CARROT CAKE

12 oz wholewheat flour
1 tsp cinnamon
4 oz ground almonds
1/2 pint walnut oil
1/2 pint soya milk

2 tsp baking powder
2 oz ground walnuts
1 1/2 lb grated carrots
4 oz date purée
8 oz maple syrup

Combine all the dry ingredients in a bowl and stir in the grated carrots. Add the remaining ingredients and pour into a medium cake tin lined with parchment paper. Bake for 45 minutes at 180°C (350°F, gas mark 4). Decorate with orange ribbon & candles as desired.

Seasonal Menu
Suggestions for your Toddler

(Suitable for all the family)

SPRING

Breakfast	Lunch	Dinner/tea
Spring refresher juice	Carrot/wheatgrass juice	Asparagus soup
Muesli	Avocado & alfalfa dip	Tofu koftas
	Rice pudding	Mixed salad leaves & sprouts

or

Breakfast	Lunch	Dinner/tea
Apple juice or Lemon Aid	Carrot/wheatgrass juice	Pasta with broad beans, peas & mint
Mashed tofu & banana	Nettle mash with carrot & celery sticks & broccoli florets	Mixed salad leaves & sprouts
Wholemeal toast with tahini	Millet pudding	

SUMMER

Breakfast	Lunch	Dinner/tea
Fruit smoothie	Pea & mint dip with pitta bread	Courgette & carrot soup
Muesli	Banana ice	Dulse & seaweed scones
		Tofu nut patties with sesame garlic dip

or

Breakfast	Lunch	Dinner/tea
Summer glory juice	Plated raw summer vegetables with guacamole	Courgette & rice cake
Mashed tofu & banana	Toasted rye bread	Sprouted lentils with Udo's oil & dulse

AUTUMN

Breakfast	Lunch	Dinner/tea
Mango & raspberry soup	Carrot & wheatgrass juice	Hemp roast with mixed salad leaves & sprouts
Soaked grains with ground seeds & apple purée	Raw houmous with carrot & celery sticks	Raspberry crumble with tofu cream
	Quinoa pilaff	

or

Breakfast	Lunch	Dinner/tea
Autumn marvel juice	Carrot & wheatgrass juice	Corn soup
Apple with date dip	Barley-vegetable casserole	Garlic mash with tomato salsa
Mixed seed grain toast	Baked banana & orange	Sprouted wheat & corn salad

WINTER

Breakfast	Lunch	Dinner/tea
Winter warmer juice	Carrot/beetroot/celery/ wheatgrass juice	Brown rice with broccoli & tofu
Banana porridge with sesame	Jacket potato with mashed avocado,	Apricot bar alfalfa & dulse

or

Breakfast	Lunch	Dinner/tea
Apple juice or Lemon Aid	Carrot/spinach/celery/ beetroot juice	Root vegetables with cornmeal crust
Couscous with coconut & mashed banana	Sweet potato soup	Date cake with tofu cream
	Millet cakes with sesame garlic dip	

How to Make your own Stocks

The flavour of all soup and grain dishes is greatly improved by using stock rather than water. Bought stock and bouillon tend to contain too much salt or other ingredients that are best avoided, like peanuts or dairy products, so read the labels carefully. It is very simple to make your own, and you can easily double the recipe and freeze some for later use.

VEGETABLE STOCK

2 onions, finely sliced
2 garlic cloves, peeled & crushed
2 medium carrots
2 outer leaves of a fennel bulb
Sprig fresh thyme
1 bay leaf

2 leek tops, chopped and washed
2 tsp dulse
2 sticks celery
6 parsley sprigs
2 fresh sage leaves
6 peppercorns

Cover the bottom of a stockpot with a little water. Add the onions, leeks, garlic and dulse and sweat very gently until soft (about 15 minutes). Add the remaining ingredients and 4 pints water, bring to the boil then gently simmer for 1 hour. Strain, pressing as much liquid as possible from the vegetables. Cool and keep covered in the fridge.

POTASSIUM BROTH

Another excellent stock to make is Potassium Broth. This can also be used as a soup or a nourishing drink. Potassium is a great healer and a great alkaliser. It aids in proper waste elimination, feeds the nerves, the heart and muscles. This is one of the best ways to neutralise unwanted acids in the body, it is also a nourishing broth to include in both your and your baby's diet.

4 medium potatoes, scrubbed & diced
4 sticks celery, diced
2 large onions, diced
1 bay leaf
Peas (mange tout if in season)

4 carrots, scrubbed & diced
4 cloves garlic, peeled & crushed
6 sprigs parsley
Sweetcorn

Finely chopped outer leaves of any or all of the following: lettuce, cauliflower, cabbage, chinese leaves, kale, etc.

Bring all the ingredients to the boil in a pot with 4 pints of water. Cover and simmer for 1 hour. Then either eat as it is or strain and use as a revitalising drink or stock.

Cooking Guide

OVEN SETTINGS & TEMPERATURES

	Celsius	Fahrenheit	Gas Mark
Slow	140	275	1
Cool	150	300	2
Warm	160	325	3
Moderate	180	350	4
	190	375	5
	200	400	6
Hot	220	425	7
Very Hot	230	450	8
	250	475	9

NB: For fan-assisted ovens, refer to the manufacturer's handbook, as times are generally reduced.

APPROXIMATE CONVERSIONS

1/2 oz	15 g
1 oz	30 g
2 oz	55 g
3 oz	85 g
4 oz	115 g
5 oz	140 g
6 oz	170 g
7 oz	195 g
8 oz	225 g
10 oz	280 g
12 oz	335 g
1 lb	450 g
1 1/4 lb	560 g
1 1/2 lb	675 g
2 lb	900 g

Information Sources

Contact details for hundreds of other food, health, organic and environmental sources, and information on organic products and stockists, organic events, organic open farms and restaurants etc., can be found in the 91-page Organic Products Directory in the companion title *The Organic Baby Book* (see below for details).

Publications

The Organic Baby Book

Why it's vital to go organic to conceive and raise a healthy baby; expert advice from leading health experts; the Foresight preconception programme; organic food, health & nutrition tips; and over 600 organic and environmentally friendly products (and their stockists) for parents, babies and young children reviewed including organic nappies, toiletries, clothing, bedding, babyfood and food supplements etc. Written by Tanyia Maxted-Frost and published by Green Books, it costs £7.95. Phone 01803 863260 or order online at <www.theorganicbabybook.co.uk>.

The Organic Directory

The indispensable national guide to help you find local, national and mail order suppliers of organic foods and services. Published by Green Books, it costs £4.95. Phone 01803 863260. (Incorporates the Soil Association's previous guide *Where to Buy Organic Food*.) The Organic Directory Online is at <www.theorganicdirectory.co.uk>.

• Other recommended general health titles include any by nutritionist Patrick Holford (Piatkus), Leslie Kenton (Ebury Press), and naturopath Jan de Vries (Mainstream).

Organisations

Fresh Network

This organisation supports anyone wanting to eat a mainly or totally raw food diet. Join to receive newsletters, a quarterly magazine, advice and more. Phone 01353 662849.

Henry Doubleday Research Association

Interested in growing your own food and want to learn how to garden organically? The HDRA, based at the Ryton Organic Gardens in Coventry, is the largest organic gardening organisation in Europe, with demonstration gardens, an organic food and book shop, and regular courses and events. Become a member to receive a regular newsletter, free entry to certain gardens, discounts on organic gardening products and other benefits. Phone 0247 6303517 or see the website at <www.hdra.org.uk>.

The Soil Association

The leading organic food charity in the UK, campaigning against GM foods, raising awareness of organic food and health issues and supporting the organic farming industry. Become a member and receive the quarterly magazine *Living Earth*. Phone 0117 929 0661 or see the website at <www.soilassociation.org>.

Penrhos Court

Regular courses on Pregnancy and Babycare, Women's Health, and Optimum Nutrition are run here in Herefordshire by Daphne Lambert. The mediaeval manor is an organic certified hotel and restaurant in the Welsh borders. Phone 01544 230720.

Juicers

The following juicers are recommended for the quality of their juice extraction and functions, and are used by the authors. They can be purchased from several juicer stockists including the Wholistic Research Company (01707 262686), Fresh Network (01353 662849) and Simply Organic (0208 545 7660).

The Champion

A large all-round juicer which can juice fruits and vegetables (not wheatgrass, however) and homogenise fruits, vegetables, nuts and sprouted seeds. Costs from £300 plus delivery.

Green Power Plus

The ultimate juicer which can do most of the things the Champion can (except homogenise fruits, nuts and sprouted seeds), and also juice wheatgrass. Costs from £400 plus delivery.

Porkert Manual Juice Extractor

This is a manual grinder which will extract juice from wheatgrass, vegetables and fruit and make purées of these, nuts and sprouted seeds. Costs from £35 plus delivery.

Green Leaf Manual Juicer
Recommended for extracting wheatgrass juice. Costs £159 from the Wholistic Research Company on 01707 262686.

Other useful products

Aquathin
Rent or buy a purifier, or buy large bottles of pure water with a tabletop or stand–alone dispenser. Phone 01784 221188. Aquathin's reverse osmosis and de-ionisation water purification systems are recommended and used by The Institute of Optimum Nutrition and The Hale Clinic.

Essential Balance
Higher Nature can provide Omega Nutrition organic oils. Ask at your local health food shop or phone 01435 882 880.

Fresh Water Filter
This plumbed-in six-stage ceramic filtration filter is recommended by leading nutritionists. Phone 0208 597 3223 or 01707 262686.

Sprouters
If you don't want to make your own try the Living Sprouts Glass Sprouting Jar with mesh lid and stand (from Simply Organic on 0208 545 7660) or the Eschenfelder Glass Sprouter (from the Wholistic Research Company on 01707 262686) which comes with two jars, mesh lids and large drainage rack and drainage tray.

Wheatgrass
Organic wheatgrass seeds are available by mail order from Planet Organic. Freeze-dried wheatgrass from Xynergy Health on 01730 813642.

Wiggly Wigglers
Make use of all those kitchen scraps by composting them for use in the garden (perhaps to grow your own food!) with an easy to use Can O Worms wormery. Call the wormline on 01981 500391.

Udo's Choice
Organic oil from Savant Distribution on 0845 0606070 or your local health food shop.

Where to buy organic food

You'll find that in order to get all the organic products you need you'll probably have to shop around. *The Organic Directory*, published by Green Books with the Soil Association, will help you do this. Try your local independent healthfood store first (ask them to order in specific products if they haven't got them), local organic box scheme or local or regional home delivery company. Also try your local farmer's market, and then, if you have one, your local organic supermarket. Shopping locally reduces traffic pollution, supports your local economy and creates local jobs.

If none of these options are available, look to a national or specialist organic home delivery company such as the ones listed in *The Organic Directory* and below (you can telephone or order online). Finally, try your supermarket—some now offer a wide range of organic goods.

Clearspring Direct
Organic, sugar-free, dairy-free and macrobiotic foods, including rice milks, Udon and Soba noodles and seaweeds, direct from the manufacturer/importer. Phone 0208 746 0152 or see their website at <www.clearspring.co.uk>.

The Green Cuisine Shop
Go online to order organic food, herbs, seeds, books, equipment and receive organic diet and ecological advice and information from the Green Cuisine Shop at Penrhos Court in Herefordshire. See the website at <www.greencuisine.org> or <www.penrhos.co.uk>, or phone 01544 230720.

Index to Main Ingredients

Index to Recipes

Your notes and recipes

If you have any wonderful recipes that you think we should include in future editions of this book, please send them to:

Daphne Lambert
Penrhos School of Health
Kington, Herefordshire HR5 3LH

or email <daphne@penrhos.co.uk>

Your notes and recipes

Your notes and recipes

Your notes and recipes

Your notes and recipes

Your notes and recipes

Your notes and recipes

Your notes and recipes

Your notes and recipes

Also available . . .

The **Organic Baby Book**

How to plan and raise a healthy child

- Why it's vital to go organic for a healthy baby
- Over 600 organic babyfoods, nappies, clothes and other products reviewed
- Organic food, health & nutrition tips

GM FREE

Tanyia Maxted-Frost

THE ORGANIC BABY BOOK

How to plan and raise a healthy child

Tanyia Maxted-Frost

"This is the book to read if you are thinking of having a baby."—*The Times*

This is the first popular guide to the benefits of an organic and GM-free wholefood diet for conceiving and raising a healthy child, and the first to review all organic products now available for your baby, for pregnant and breastfeeding mothers, and for young families. *The Organic Baby Book*, which features advice from leading health experts including Patrick Holford and Leslie Kenton, shows that it is now possible to eat, drink and buy nearly everything needed for mother and baby organically: fresh organic wholefoods • organic cotton reusable nappies • ready-made babyfoods • cot blankets • bras and nursing pads • baby clothing • bodycare • food supplements • bedding • toys • and more.

Over 600 organic and environmentally-friendly products, companies, relevant organisations, annual events and useful resources are reviewed. The book also features: the experiences of parents who have gone organic and reaped the rewards • how to 'green' your house for your baby • and the vaccination versus healthy immune system debate.

Tanyia Maxted-Frost is a former London journalist specialising in organic food and health issues. She is now Managing Editor of the Australian magazine *Homes & Living*. **Green Books 160pp ISBN 1 870098 79 X £7.95 paperback**

Order through your local green retailer or high street bookseller, or from The Organic Baby Book website at:

www.theorganicbabybook.co.uk

In case of difficulty, please order direct from Green Books:

Tel: 01803 863260   Fax: 01803 863843
sales@greenbooks.co.uk   www.greenbooks.co.uk

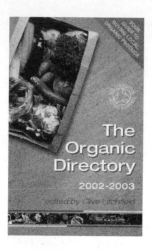